Offerings:
The Decluttering of a Life

Offerings:
The Decluttering of a Life

by

Kathleen A. Dale

To Anne
with love
Kathleen
Dec 2019
thanks for the
sharing
about our
lives!

ISBN-13: 978-1-7337114-0-1

Zarigueya
Press

zarigueyapress.com

Other Works by Kathleen A. Dale

Poetry
(available from the author at *kathleenanndale.com*):

Ties that Bind (Finishing Line Press, 2006)
Rescue Mission (Antrim House, 2011)
Avatars of Baubo (Green Fuse Poetic Arts, 2013)
The Beautiful Unnamed (Zarigueya Press, 2015)

Children's Book:

Deconstruction Zone (Lulu Publishing, 2012)

Recitals of Piano Works by Contemporary Women:

https://www.soundcloud.com/kathleenann45

for those who have also sought answers
and thereby created meaning

Notes and Acknowledgements

This book has been several years in the making. Based on twenty-seven volumes of my journals from ages sixteen to present, it was an enormous task to sort through them and to decide on which areas to focus. Ultimately, it became clear that several themes—childhood trauma and grief, creativity, spirituality, family relationships, being female—were all present and intricately related.

Some names have been changed to protect privacy. All pictures or photographs are from family archives or pixabay.com.

First, I would like to thank the members of my long-time writing group—Louisa Loveridge Gallas, Judith Harway, and Bill Murtaugh—for their generous suggestions about ways to winnow my various drafts (including the penultimate one) into a readable, coherent manuscript.

Thanks also to Patricia Wingate Gonet and Deborah Fries for reading parts of the manuscript at different stages and providing insightful and helpful feedback.

More than I can say, I appreciate the many readers who commented on the content as I published this book online, chapter by chapter, from October, 2018, through early March, 2019. Relating your experiences to my own changed this book for the better as I continually revised. Though the online chapters are now gone, the Facebook discussion group (women only) will continue for a time. If you would like to join the discussion:
https://www.facebook.com/Groups/Offerings.

Acknowledgements of works referenced in each chapter are listed at the end of the book under "References." The author of each work listed there has unknowingly helped to make my own journey a bit easier knowing that I have never been alone in asking the questions that I do.

Finally, to my family: my husband, here called Ben, the love of my life, who arrived at just the right *time* in my life and who has always supported all that was important to me; to our amazing and wonderfully unique daughters, who tell their own stories best; and to our two grandsons, who always bring out the mischievous kid in me again.

I would like more sisters, that the taking out of one might not leave such stillness.
　　　　　—Emily Dickinson, Letter 200, February, 1859

Nothing has a stronger influence psychologically on their environment and especially on their children than the unlived life of the parent.

　　　　　—C.G. Jung, Collected Works, Vol. XVI

Contents

One:

Just Say the Words; then You Can Go Play the Piano

He didn't know what to do with me. My heart was racing, my palms were sweaty, my stomach hurt, and I could not look him in the eye. My frightened mother had made this appointment for me with the "youth minister" in preparation for my confirmation in the Methodist Church the following Sunday because I had finally told her that I didn't want to take the seven vows I would have to profess.

It was 1957, and even then, my twelve-year-old self knew that I could not stand in front of the congregation and "just say" that I was there "To renounce the spiritual forces of wickedness, reject the evil powers of the world, and repent of my sin; To receive and profess the Christian faith as contained in the Scriptures of the Old and New Testaments"; or that I planned "To be loyal to Christ through The United Methodist Church and do all in my power to strengthen its ministries."

All of the words I was supposed to say demanded belief. Words, I thought, mattered, and the idea that I would have to say them as if I actually believed them made me feel physically sick.

Was I really a "sinner"? Was the world really so "evil"? Was everything in the Bible literally true? If so, why did God let my sister die? What about those raised in other religions like my Jewish friend Doreen? Would she go to hell?

As someone raised in the Bible Belt of central Kansas in the first part of the twentieth century, my mother was deeply disturbed by what she saw as my stubbornness: she probably thought I was in danger of losing my immortal soul. But I don't think she was much more distraught than were the associate minister and I by this enforced tête-à-tête. I was clearly a first for him. He fiddled with his glasses as I sat across from his big desk. "So what's going on?" he asked with a worried frown. When I finally mumbled out my "doubts," he let out a big sigh and said, smiling, "Don't worry about it. Just do what everyone else does. Just say the words." He got up from his desk; the interview was over.

I was initially relieved, and fled from his office to my mother's waiting car. And I did recite the required words the following Sunday. But something about what he had said bothered me. Did words themselves have no real meaning? Though so far I had written only a little poetry, one had been published in the now-defunct magazine of the Girl Scouts, called *American Girl*. As I recall, I wrote simply about the immediate, physical pleasures of summer—cherry popsicles, bathing suits on the line (though I had not yet learned how to swim). In the year I turned 16—the age at which my sister had died—I started a private journal in a spiral-bound school notebook. It begins, "Recently I have become aware that I am growing up—am becoming a person—an individual with my own ideas and opinions on things. I want to grow into the kind of person I should be—one who is untouched by conformity

2

and mediocrity—one who is able to let his [sic] mind wander and soar—think about the basic questions of life. I am hoping that this journal will aid in this growth." [Today it is mind-boggling to think that for the first quarter century of my life, women were referred to by the pronoun "he" when spoken of collectively, as human beings.] I end the first entry with a kind of self-conscious flourish: "This book will have served its purpose if it leads me into a better understanding of myself and what I stand for, the world around me and my God, and what I am going to do with my life."

In my journal, I copied down passages from books I liked (*Our Town, A Tree Grows in Brooklyn*, and *The Edge of Tomorrow* by the tropical doctor named Thomas Dooley). "Is life merely a search?" I wrote at the end of my sixteenth year. "A search for the better, always moving out beyond what one can comprehend? The other day while stirring a pan of beans on the stove the miracle of just being—living and feeling—came upon me."

But I never shared my journal or its thoughts with anyone. I knew that my parents would be made anxious by my questioning, and my father had told me never to mention my sister to my mother because it was too painful for her to talk about (something she much later—too late—denied).

We wrote essays in high school, of course. I was a good writer and a good student overall, but sadly, that was the death knell for a girl's popularity in 1962. Many girls planned to go to college, but only to get teaching or nursing degrees until they got married, which was the main goal. I graduated seventh in a class of 700 and was embarrassed that my peers knew I had done so well. As a junior, I had the opportunity to switch to a more challenging AP English class but refused, partly because I was trying to fit in with the academically "average" but "popular" crowd, and partly because I had a crush on the unmotivated but cute boy who sat across the aisle from me. Frustrated, my teacher asked me to enter a contest in which I was to write my autobiography. I had written a fairly conventional autobiography in ninth grade, but didn't want to do anything similar this time. I finally agreed, but turned in only a one-page metaphor of how my life was an uncertain trip in a very small boat, following a dim light that I eventually hoped would lead me to somewhere that would finally reveal the meaning of life. My English teacher *begged* me to write a more conventional autobiography but I refused. The metaphorical image was, to me, truer to who I actually was than all the outer events that had "occurred" to me so far in my short life.

My sister Marilyn had also written a rather conventional autobiography in the ninth grade (it must be a standard requirement to look back at your life from that vantage point). Hers, like mine at that age, was the predictable recounting of what she had been told of her birth, what she remembered from her school years, the death of our grandmother—whom she knew but I couldn't remember—, the move to Wichita when she was 15 and I was five, and her hopes to be a teacher or a journalist someday. She wanted to go to Southern Methodist University, while my mother wanted her to stay closer to home.

Though I kept disappointing my English teacher, I continued to write, secretly, in my journal. "What is time?" I asked. "How long do I have here—50 or 60 years? or maybe only 20 or 30—but think of the endless stretch of time before we were born and after we die. Perhaps now we are being trained for another life. But one thing is certain—we will never again live in a material world. Once after we leave we will never again see a hair, the sky, the sun, a tree, peach jam, a car, clothes, dogs, lightbulbs, doorknobs, the white of milk in a glass, a daisy, the fizz of a coke." What I couldn't even voice in my journal was that, like my sister and like Sleeping Beauty, I believed that I too would die at 16. Hence it was even more urgent to "get right with God." But my concept of God was changing even as I wrote about it: "I believe that there is a great force behind all things—a great force that IS all things. I believe that there is a meaning and a pattern to everything. I believe that every life has a purpose and I believe that someday one will be shown to me. I believe that communication is possible with this force and is experienced by each person—each in his [sic] own way." This spontaneous profession of belief was a far cry from the confirmation "vows" I recited by rote at age twelve, where there had been absolutely no room for doubt, ambiguity, or qualification— elements which, I later discovered, were essential, not only to poetry, but to the act of thinking itself.

* * *

I had been harshly taught that things could end quite suddenly, irrevocably, without warning. Just as Persephone was pulled underground by Pluto one afternoon while innocently picking daisies, the sister I idolized died suddenly in late August, 1952. The polio virus hit on a Saturday night. She was taking care of me while my parents were out celebrating their anniversary. She said she felt ill, and by morning they took her to the emergency ward. She rapidly got worse and had trouble swallowing and breathing. Since it was Sunday, the nurses could not reach a doctor who would authorize her move to an iron lung. So she died that afternoon with my parents beside her, while I was still waiting, alone, all day, in our car in the hospital parking lot, children not being allowed in the hospital. I never got to say goodbye. I didn't understand what "passed away" meant when they told me.

The 1952 polio epidemic in America killed over three thousand children, leaving tens of thousands crippled. Marilyn was one of the unlucky 3,145. Once upon a time, I had a sister, Marilyn, born in 1935, nearly ten years older than I. My mother had several miscarriages before and between our births. I adored Marilyn. I followed her everywhere. I asked for an extra piece of birthday cake for her whenever I was invited to a party. I drew pictures for her. She taught me finger games. I was jealous of the other kids she babysat.

I was not yet born when she had her first bout with the polio that crippled one of her legs. While she was still a child, the surgeons broke and shortened her other leg so that her limp wouldn't be so pronounced. Nevertheless, she still limped, and her left leg was much less developed than her right. Still, she was active, and never let that handicap keep her from horseback-riding (her passion), dancing, swimming, or playing tennis.

It was not yet known that there were different strains of the polio virus, ranging from the crippler to the killer. Since my sister had had a mild, but crippling, form of the disease several years earlier, everyone thought she was immune when this new outbreak in 1952 began, so in late August she freely drank at water fountains and swam in the suspect city pools. Everyone was then horrified to discover that she had succumbed to the worst strain, the one that paralyzes lungs, just days before her senior year in high school was to begin. All this I was told later. I have since thought that, physically active as she was, despite her crippled leg and hands, she would have hated facing life in an iron lung. My mother's journal revealed that Marilyn had always been afraid of having to live most of her life in an iron lung. So, as someone who is similarly active, I do understand that, for her, death may have been the best option (not that she had a choice).

Marilyn's death brought to the forefront the mood disorders that had been lurking in our family. Unfortunately, anxiety and depression existed on both sides of my parents' families. Such relatives were referred to as being "high strung" or "nervous" and were often told just to "calm down" and not to "take things so seriously." Certainly our family doctor never considered drugs for my or my father's anxiety or my mother's anxiety and depression, which became disabling after the death of her firstborn. Since my father had told me never to talk to my mother about Marilyn, I never spoke of her at all—to anyone—and no one else did either. Her vibrant, living self thus began to fade from my memory. I developed terrible stomach cramps (Irritable Bowel Syndrome had not yet been recognized), a multitude of skin problems, and chronic insomnia. I associated "going to sleep"

6

with death and had to ask my mother a series of questions like "Will I still swallow while I'm asleep?" every night for several years following my sister's death. (I knew that my sister had died because her throat had closed up.) The "legacy" prayer passed down mother to mother for decades did not help: "Now I lay me down to sleep/I pray the Lord my soul to keep./If I should die before I wake/I pray the Lord my soul to take." I say "legacy" because within my mother's and certainly my grandmothers' memories were many children's deaths endured time and again before there were vaccines for diphtheria and whooping cough and measles.

The Salk vaccine against polio came out in 1955 when I was ten. I remember my mother, father, and I standing in line to take one of the vaccine-soaked sugar cubes. Of course, then, as well as today, there was talk about how the vaccine itself could cause the dreaded disease. But most people feared the disease so much that they took their chances. I have a memory snapshot of my father picking up a sugar cube, looking at it a moment, pausing, and then nonchalantly popping it into his mouth.

Though anxiety was rampant in our family as well as widespread in America during the 1950s and 60s, the only drugs to treat it at the time were meprobamate (Miltowns) or diazepam (Valium), and neither was ever prescribed to any member of my remaining family. My father, however, smoked three packs of cigarettes a day (nicotine calms), and our home was always filled with its smell. My parents didn't touch alcohol because, not only were we Methodists, which forbid drinking, but Kansas was (and still is) a "dry" state. There seemed to be no remedy.

When someone suggested that I might benefit from therapy, my father roared, "There's nothing wrong with her mind!" In terms of treating the "common colds" of mental illness—anxiety and depression—few, if anyone, knew what they were doing in the 1950s, the "age of anxiety" as W.H. Auden termed it, when nuclear war was supposedly imminent during the "Cold War" between Russia and the United States.

In the seventh grade, I wrote a story about Wichita, headquarters for the manufacture of Boeing B-52s, being hit by a nuclear bomb that wiped out our entire family. When my teacher read it aloud in class, I squirmed in my seat, but was secretly pleased. Our family, of course, *had* been hit by something like a nuclear bomb, and I think now that my teacher's acknowledgement of the feeling behind the story was in some small way affirming, if not healing.

In the early 2000s I created a website about Marilyn— scanning in family snapshots, poems I had written, photos of things I gave her or that belonged to her. I included information about polio today, about the progress being made toward its eradication. I didn't want to become obsessed with it but I wanted some "gold" to be separated from all that leaden sorrow. We are never completely free of the past, though we can create with it. I published the website, and several close friends and family members responded. Over time, T.S. Eliot's *The Wasteland* with its underlying Fisher King mythology and war-time references eventually helped me to start asking the "right" though unanswerable questions: What went wrong? Why do some live to learn and express their potential and others do not? Why do some come to flower and others shrivel on the vine?

Cleaning out my dresser drawer recently, I found, pushed to the back, two items belonging to my sister: the 1950s sheer gloves she wore to church (much too small for my hands) and a coin purse with the last baby-sitting money she ever made during the summer of 1952.

* * *

Pema Chödrön's *Living Beautifully with Uncertainty and Change* (2013) recalls my therapist's advice about relinquishing fixed "stories" about ourselves, our lives, and the lives of others, accepting the "groundlessness of radical freedom." Stories can be helpful only if we realize that they are *fictions*, but, too often, we become spell-bound by them.

My therapists have always been quick to point this out in the repeated "story" I tell about my sister's death. "What do you gain by holding on to it?" they ask. Good question. Gradually, over time, I have found myself loosening the "stories" of my past, and the complex, knotted, painful connections that I have made with them.

I have found that focusing on "variations" both in my writing and in my music helps. Old stories fall away to be replaced by other stories, but with longer and longer stretches of silence, of possibility, between them. Since the sudden death of my sister more than 65 years ago, I have written more than 40 poems about her, each in a different way trying to work through the experience I didn't know how to handle at age seven. My therapist finally drew me a picture representing the alchemy of healing: one continues to repeat/replay the same story over and over again until one day, some piece of it changes, and one escapes through that crevice.

* * *

When I was about 11, my parents and I drove to San Diego, California, to visit relatives and friends who had moved there during the Great Depression. While there we visited the relatively new Hale telescope at Mt. Palomar, named after George Ellery Hale, the astronomer who created the 200" Palomar reflector, the most important telescope in the world between 1949 and 1992. In a 1928 letter seeking funding for his project, Hale wrote: "No method of advancing science is so productive as the development of new and more powerful instruments and methods of research. A larger telescope would not only furnish the necessary gain in light space-penetration and photographic resolving power, but permit the application of ideas and devices derived chiefly from the recent fundamental advances in physics and chemistry." The telescope was built and dedicated to Hale, who also suffered from severe depression, in 1948.

We drove to the giant dome of the observatory, about two hours from San Diego, and climbed the 70 steps to the telescope. While we couldn't, of course, look through the telescope itself, we could look at the many photographs that had been painstakingly taken of the known universe in 1956. When we came out, after looking at the dark and gigantic universe, I realized that, indeed (as I had suspected), there was no "heaven": only a vast, empty and lonely universe, through which we were endlessly falling. Riding back to our motel in the backseat of our big Buick (without seatbelts), I felt sick to my stomach.

No one I knew ever had any immediate, visceral, meaningful ritual that helped to mitigate the adolescent/human anxiety that comes with the foreknowledge of death. I had no one who showed the way or who accompanied me on my quest. Not being able to speak my sister's name or voice my own doubts about orthodoxy because they caused my mother so much pain was the kind of enforced silence that turned inward and festered.

I did not know it, but I was *not* alone. It is generally known that the 1950s were a time of anxiety and regression for women in general: the average age at which women married dropped, and fewer women went to college. Post-war consumer culture spread the myth that fulfillment for a woman was found in the home, as a wife and mother. It was common to find that women were unhappy because their choices were limited; they were expected to make a "career" out of being housewives and mothers, excluding all other pursuits. Betty Friedan, in her research that culminated in *The Feminine Mystique* (1963), noted the unhappiness of many housewives who were trying to fit this feminine mystique image, and she called the widespread uneasiness "the problem that has no name."

I had never heard of Betty Friedan as a senior in high school in 1963, but this is what I wrote in my journal: "I know that I want to marry and have children, but this is not what I have been educated for. I have been educated in dimensions

10

of the mind, not detergent. I have been taught of great literature and chemistry, not soap-box TV serials and burned TV dinners. Living the rest of my life with children would be dull—I would not accomplish anything that anyone over 14 couldn't do. I want to contribute to society—to create, to fulfill and stretch my mind, soul, and imagination during my *whole life*—not to have it completed and over with after the birth of a child. I am a woman, yes—but I am also a human being, and as such must search and explore this earth and work all my days so that I can find my identity and establish a firm lasting, creative personality with a positive and contributing relationship with the world, with my family, with myself, and with God."

A tall order. And I would continue for years, in my journal, the practice of the self-repudiation I had mouthed during my confirmation: renouncing "sins" like "selfishness, impatience, unfeelingness and insensitivity to the needs and desires of others, self-pity." Women at that time were to cultivate the very opposite qualities: patience, self-abnegation, and attention to the needs of others.

In the decade between seven and seventeen, I slowly worked through—by myself—first, in my body and then in the alchemical process of my journal, my feelings about what had happened to my beloved sister: the one who had loved me, who took me everywhere, played games with me, showed me off to everyone, let me sit behind her holding tight around her waist when she went horseback riding, who never told me I was a nuisance, and was my second, much calmer mother. I did not understand what had happened. Even as I saw her at the funeral home, I told people that she was not really dead: that I could see her move. A few days later I started second grade. I never cried until much, much later. I was too busy learning how to survive, and how to atone for the guilt of survival.

* * *

Aside from my journal, the piano became my second alchemist. The September after my sister's death, I coincidentally had my first piano lesson. Like many families of the mid-twentieth century, we had a piano—at first an old upright, but later, a Baldwin spinet. My mother and sister both played piano. My mother's family of origin could never afford real lessons, but my mother had a good ear and could play a few hymns that she loved. My sister took lessons in Stafford, and when she first had polio, would "practice" by drumming her fingers on the blanket (she later played the snare drum for the high school marching band even though one leg was shorter than the other and her hands were shrunken because of the unsuccessful x-ray treatments she had undergone).

I started lessons with a neighborhood woman who gave lessons at her house. For seven years, Mrs. Lebow showed me the joys of creative expression that come with discipline. I never had to be told to practice. I was at the piano every day after school until my father came home from work and turned on the television. I felt cherished by Mrs. Lebow and basked in the belief that I was her favorite student.

When I was about 14, Mrs. Lebow said that she had no more to teach me and referred me to the head of the piano department at Wichita State University, where I took lessons until I left for college. Dr. Steinbauer pushed me even harder, expanding my repertoire to more modern (all-male) composers, and showing me off to his college students, asking them why they couldn't apply themselves as I was doing? Indeed, he "puffed me up" until I foresaw a career on the concert stage.

As a senior in high school, I had to give a completely memorized, hour-long recital of compositions by Mozart, Beethoven, Bartok, Prokofiev, and others. Before the recital, I was sick with nervousness. When my memory failed me during one of the later pieces, I simply had to stop and abandon the rest of the recital. My humiliation was like nothing I had ever known. I had failed, miserably. Shortly after, Dr. Steinbauer finally told me the truth: that I would make a good teacher, but not a professional performer. So then and there I decided to stop playing. I didn't want to teach or to play the organ for the Church as my mother wanted, but whose concept of God I had come to abhor.

I would become a doctor instead. I would heal people like my sister.

Family Snapshot

You sit at the center:
the older sister,
the only one of us smiling,
the only one composed, gazing
direct into the eye of the camera
as if to affirm (though the rest
    of us
won't know this for another
    month):
your life stands complete.

The rest of us are caught
somewhere in the midst of our lives,
perched on the porch steps
(despite cracks in the cement).
We are blurred or blinking or glancing off
at the horizon or down at the dogs.
We have so many more things
to do. We can hardly wait to
shift, to be released from this enforced
immobility.

Grouped in still life, no one looks
at anyone else. No one touches. Un-posed,
we suffer the shot in the thick of our
own separate, suspended lives.

Though we didn't see it then,
it's clear as the sky before a quake:
you were to become the core of our epic,
your approaching death
(forever after) our epicenter.

Two:

College and My Various Initiations

My Kappa Kappa Gamma sorority paddle, highly polished and engraved with the Kappa crest, was never used to hit me; however, such paddles were long used in both fraternity and sorority houses for spanking and other forms of hazing. Mine now lies deep in a closet along with yearbooks and some of my other souvenirs from my college years, waiting for me to decide what to do with them.

In early September of 1963, I drove with my parents the hundreds of miles "back East" to Ohio Wesleyan University, where I had been accepted as a freshman. We had attended church the previous week in Stafford, where I was born. After the service, one of my parents' acquaintances collared me on the church steps and said, "Why are you leaving your parents like this? You'll just come back thinking that you're better than all the rest of us." I smiled sweetly, as usual, and kept silent as I always did when I knew meaningful communication was impossible.

The first thing we did on moving-in-day —a Sunday— was of course to go to church. Then we met my roommate and her family from Buffalo, New York. I unpacked. There was a dinner and convocation for freshmen and parents that evening after which we said goodbye—hardest for my mother, I'm sure. She left, reassured because we all had to go to "chapel" three mornings a week. What she didn't know was that attendance was taken by means of turning in IBM cards, which your roommate could easily do for you and you for her if one of you had had an exceptionally late night or simply didn't want to go.

The last night of freshman move-in weekend was a "retreat" at a place called Camp Christian. That night I wrote, "I met a few nice girls and got quite a few looks from boys but no offers. Boys worry me now. I wish I didn't act so shy."

The ensuing semester was one of the happiest times of my life. I lost some of my shyness. Even President Kennedy's assassination in November didn't burst my "happy bubble." I was "rushed" by the "best" sorority on campus (Kappa Kappa Gamma), honored for my grade point average (which kept the sorority's average high), and was soon "pinned" to the president of Sigma Chi. No one knew that I had been a nerdy wallflower who had hid my intelligence in high school. I now wore contacts instead of cat-eye glasses and had a stylish bouffant (helmeted) hairdo! I had an "engaged-to-be-engaged" boyfriend (with whom I was doing "everything but") and a whole SET of new "sisters" to replace the one who had abandoned me. I even had a new "big sister" who was to show me how things were best done at OWU. Kathy was a senior pre-med student, so I only knew her one year, but she left me a copy of a beautiful book of photographs called *The Family of Man* [sic] in which she wrote, "I expect great things from you." It was music to my ears.

16

At college, most of my "nervous" symptoms magically disappeared, except for occasional migraine headaches, which blinded and nauseated me, and sent me to my bed for a couple of days a month. And I sometimes had nightmares from which I always awoke feeling accused and guilty.

My first science course on my pre-med schedule, microbiology, was a big disappointment: I was uncomfortable with the necessary exactness in the endless experiments and had a lot of trouble becoming interested in the point of them. In science, it seemed that there was always just ONE right answer, recalling my discomfort at the "only" correct answers in my religious education. Perhaps for opposite reasons, I was enamored with my English writing and literature classes. I had placed out of freshman English by taking AP English in high school, but my college advanced composition teacher made it clear that I should NOT have been excused from English 1. My writing was sloppy and undisciplined, and Dr. Ruth Davies held me to higher standards than anyone else ever had (except my childhood piano teachers). When she handed back my first essay in "Advanced Composition" covered with red marks, I was shocked! My pride was a little injured, but at least she cured me of all those dashes with which I had punctuated my journal up until that point. I finally "got" the point of organization and structure, though I am still not overly organized in many areas of my life.

Dr. Benjamin Spencer was my other favorite English teacher. He would stand at the front of the fourth-floor room in an old hall, with ancient desks and an uneven wooden floor, reading Walt Whitman's "Out of the Cradle Endlessly Rocking." I would be so engrossed, he later told me, that a bomb might have gone off in the back of the room and I would not have noticed. We also read Dickinson that semester, but I was never brave enough in Dr. Davies' class to imitate Emily's dashes.

Ruth Davies was my first female academic role model; I'd never known anyone like her. She was in her 50s, never married as far as we could tell, but had traveled all over the world, especially to Russia (she also taught Russian literature in which, of course, I also enrolled). She never hesitated to speak her mind, so her feedback was honest and soon became welcome. No one had ever before suggested that my writing or reading skills left room for improvement. This was indeed an initiation! Furthermore, she wore amazing clothes in groupings of reds and purples, a combination I still admire and occasionally wear myself.

I was being intellectually challenged for the first time in my life; I had the freedom to think unconventional thoughts and to do pretty much what I liked with my days; I was frequently asked out on dates—to "barn parties" where I had my first taste of liquor, which I didn't much like. I smoked, like everyone else, and because my father had expressly forbidden it. Though Kappas could smoke, they were never to be seen walking down the street in an un-lady-like manner with a lit cigarette. I had roommates and sorority "sisters." Life was grand, aside from the weekly call I had to make home to my parents, in which, as usual, nothing much was revealed, especially by me. They would never have approved of my college life!

Women did not live in their sorority houses, though men who were members of fraternities could live in their fraternity houses. All women lived in dormitories and had a ten p.m. curfew (a little later on the weekends). As members of "Greek" organizations, we wore togas during our rituals that paid lip-service to our "mission" of service to the community. There were secret handshakes, secret votes, all meant to exclude outsiders. During rush, a "rush-ee" could be "black-balled" by anyone who did not want her for *any* reason. Once accepted, however, we felt ourselves to be truly "special": the old practice of actually "paddling" Greek organization initiates was no longer done (at least in the sororities).

However, one of my sorority sisters, in the same class as I, recently described this scenario that I was not aware of until she wrote to me:

Right after we pledged we were having a meeting with a national KKG rep talking to us about history, the joy of being a Kappa, etc. Someone (can't remember who) asked if it was true that black girls were not allowed. The National woman explained that our Kappa sisters would be our best friends for the rest of our lives and that our parents would not want us to have a black best friend. I spoke up and said that one of my best friends was black and that my parents were fine with that. (That was not totally true - I did have a black best friend, but I was only allowed to go to her house; she couldn't come to mine because my mother was worried about what the neighbors would think - we had great big fights about that.) Anyway, right after that, the National woman expressed to the house leadership that I should be dropped because of this. One of the leaders, a junior, told me about this and said that she was taking a stand and that if I was asked to leave she would quit too. I almost wanted to quit right then, but she specifically asked me not to. Instead I had to have lunch every week for some months with this stupid woman. Each week I had to sit there and listen to her "rehabilitate" me. I learned to sit quietly and put up with her. I think I had very mixed emotions - I hated the lunches, but also I disliked the idea of not being in that very good sorority, and I had some feeling for our president, who was such a standup young woman.

Another one of our pledge sisters told the following story, decades after the fact: her mother was Jewish, which of course makes her legally Jewish although the family didn't identify that way. Our Kappa chapter wanted to pledge her, but Jews were not allowed at the time. She was asked not to reveal her maternal heritage. Therefore "National" was not told and so our chapter was able to "sneak" her in.

Today, my sorority sister writes, "What gets me about her story, and mine as well, is that both of us were willing to deny our principles in order to be in a sorority. The social pressure was strong enough to make us behave in very shameful ways - or at least I did." We were metaphorically "paddled" into accepting the strict rules for membership, for belonging, even though I thought I had left all such coercion back in Kansas.

My lack of political awareness persisted, perhaps because of such enforced secrecy. I was vaguely aware of the Civil Rights Act passed by Congress in 1964, but did not connect it to events occurring on my own campus. According to the OWU website, "In 1964 the Board of Trustees adopted a policy requiring all campus organizations to eliminate discriminatory membership clauses."

The Tri-Deltas, our next-door sorority, were first to test the new law. As one person recalls, "The Tri-Delts pledged a black girl, beautiful, very smart, in the ROTC 'Angel Flight.' National went berserk, but the chapter stayed firm. So when it came time for the pledge test they sent a very difficult and unusual test and all the pledges failed it. Of course, they were allowed to have a second chance and everyone studied the pledge manual very carefully and the second test was even harder than the first - the only person who passed it was the black girl, so National gave up and the third test was the regular easy one and everyone was activated."

Though I didn't know about any of these events at the time, I remember becoming very disillusioned after my freshman year with the exclusivity of our sorority. But I never had the nerve to leave it. In a letter from Boston during September of my sophomore year, my former "big sister" Kathy, now a pre-med student, wrote, "Rush is cruel and superficial and silly. There is no doubt about this for one who thinks about it. Besides abolishing the system, the only way I know to combat this is to make a genuine effort to look below the surface of every personality that you meet. Insist that others do the same. The whole rush set-up, indeed, even sororities in general, are things one HAS to think about, get upset over, and then decide whether to get out or work within their framework. There is no one answer." She also said, tactfully, on the announcement of my being "pinned," "I never regret having been pinned or having waited until I was a junior to do it. But this again is strictly an individual matter. No matter what decisions you make or don't make, I have great confidence in you." These latter words were ones that, as an uninitiated virgin, I needed desperately to hear.

In 2015, Ohio Wesleyan was ranked 56th out of 880 colleges in terms of being politically liberal. However, during my tenure there, that was still to come. The demonstrations against ROTC (I was also a proud marching member of its "Angel Flight") and for a Women's Studies Department took place in the years after I had left. The only black faces I ever saw on campus belonged to a few (male) Nigerian students. In 1963 it might as well have been 1953 in terms of OWU's social culture.

My parents were against my joining a sorority, not because of its exclusivity, but because it cost quite a bit of money. (Ultimately, I agreed to earn the money myself by working summers as a full-time cashier at a small grocery store near our home, where I was "teased"—sexually harassed—by the male workers every single day.) My family had no experience with such social organizations, with the exception of the Masons and Eastern Star, both Christian organizations with esoteric/occult roots and a lot of ritual that I'm sure the Methodist church looked down upon. John Wesley did not believe in ritual of any kind, considering it Papist. But I believe that most human beings long for the sensuousness and immediacy of ritual, which can indeed help propel the participant from the mundane to another level of experience, especially when words fail. As a senior in high school, I had briefly visited other churches, in search of what I felt missing. Perhaps predictably, the Episcopalian church (of 1962) appealed to me the most with its incense, participation of the congregation, and the poetic/lyrical cadences of the Book of Common Prayer. Perhaps it was such experiences that my parents and most of their friends sought in the Masonic Temple. Though nominally "Christian," the original Masons had borrowed heavily from the Occult with its own sensuous, participatory rituals and initiations. Later in my life I would be drawn to the feminist resurgence of Wicca, with its beautiful, female-centered rituals in which we did more than sit demurely in pews with our ankles crossed.

In high school I was persuaded by my parents to be a member of the "Rainbow Girls," open only to daughters of Masons. We had colorful, ritual-filled meetings in which we were assigned revolving initiatory roles such as "Faith," "Hope," and "Charity," and the seven "Rainbow" stations, which included the feared Death/Immortality (green): "The understanding that death is a part of life," which of course I already knew. But I never became close to any of the other members, who all went to different schools, and with whom I had little else in common.

There were no black members in any of these organizations, either in Kansas or in Ohio. I never went to school with black students and none of my teachers were black. There were no black members of our church. My father regularly referred to Brazilian nuts as "nigger toes" and often referred derisively to the poorer part of Wichita as "nigger town." When some dark-skinned people moved across the street from us while I was away at college, my father called to say he was somewhat relieved that they were East Indians, not "niggers."

Once or twice I tried to talk with my father about his racism, but he always got angry, asking me if that was "what I was learning back East in college," and citing "evidence" that black people were "shiftless," "lazy," etc.: all the old Jim Crow stereotypes that he had grown up with. Once again, there was no real conversation in our family about a significant topic. Enforced silence about such subjects ruled.

*   *   *

I had a scare during the second semester of my freshman year. I found a lump in my left breast and had to fly home, not to have it biopsied as would be done six times later in my life, but to have it surgically removed. Even though found to be benign, its very occurrence was still another initiation: more evidence that happiness was fleeting and that death could come at any time as it had for my sister, no matter how happy I seemed to be. Similarly, my heady romance with the Sigma Chi president declined toward the end of my freshman year. I wanted a loving husband, but also more. I wanted to be an individual, and I believed that most married women gave that up when they married, though Jacqueline Kennedy, with all of her own money and education, seemed to be an exception. I was so easily swayed by my surroundings—the patterns of those around me. Ultimately I thought it was OK to settle for sex and good manners. Unfortunately, the Sigma Chi was a "neat-nik" and, on one of the few occasions when men were allowed in our dorm rooms (door opened), he discovered a dirty potato salad bowl that I had not yet washed. He also pointed out that I "wasted" toothpaste by squeezing the tube in the middle. He was no doubt judging me by the standards for the wife he hoped I would someday become, but that was the beginning of the "end" for me. In my journal I wrote, "Love should be easy, natural. I guess man [sic], or in particular me, isn't capable of the easy kind—it is hard work to understand for a change instead of being understood. Is what I *am* good enough, or must I change to be loved? Should I be true to my messy, disorganized self? I personally believe human things—intangibles—are worth more than all the wasted toothpaste and dirty potato salad bowls cluttering up the beautiful: *Gershwin* is important; *life* is important; books are important. Not perfection and neatness, but attempts and dissonance."

As I recall, I was not very kind when I ended it. I probably said something very similar to what I wrote above. I was neither very articulate nor very honest. What I didn't say was that I had my eye on someone new—a fellow English major in the fraternity with the worst reputation on campus—the SAEs—the "animal house." Unlike the tall, preppy, blond

Sigma Chi, Luke was dark, with lots of curly brown hair, a devilish laugh, and loved to mis-quote Dostoyevsky's Raskolnikov: "Am I to get married simply for the sake of the furniture?" He had a good sense of humor and, like me, seemed to want more out of life than what his upper-middle-class parents had "settled for."

Ultimately we did get "pinned" in our sophomore year and married the year after I earned the master's degree that would allow me to put him through the University of Chicago Law School, though his parents of course paid the expensive tuition. Both of our "initiation paddles" hung proudly in our new home.

Now in a crawl space in our present home with my third husband, the beautiful, polished oak paddle branded with the name of Kappa as well as the names of me and many of my soon-to-be-forgotten "sisters" lies in a box with some of my academic papers from both college and graduate school. Though I see myself as one who can still be "initiated" into many further "mysteries," I plan to sell the paddle on eBay (average price $25) or, more likely, carry the paddle out to the curb, along with a few of my surviving college papers, the "mysteries" of which I now more or less understand.

Three:

She Encounters Failure, Seduction, and Her Capacity to Betray

Now, in May of '68, about to be married to Luke, the second boy I was pinned to in college, I wrote, "In six weeks I shall be married. If there's one thing I've learned in eight years, it's that certainty and security are never quite within one's grasp. One can only close one's eyes and jump when you are not sure what's ahead. Love makes it easier but somehow love itself becomes the problem, for ultimately what we do and what becomes of us is so intimately tied up with whom we love. I kept this journal as a young girl looking for a self, the real person who is me. When one marries, one partially gives up that individual self in favor of becoming part of a larger self. I wonder if I'm ready and if this is what I really want."

I obviously had doubts, but just as before, I went along with what was expected.

Our wedding was not a joyous occasion. Only a few people attended since all of our college friends were hundreds of miles away. I dressed in the "Bride's Room," which had been donated to the church by my parents. They dedicated it, of course, to the memory of Marilyn. Standing before the minister after my father "gave me away," I did not give much thought to the traditional vows Luke and I were repeating. After all, I had been told, just over a decade earlier, that church-written vows were "just words." Therefore, I dutifully parroted back the lines the minister fed me. My favorite aunt was the only one to throw rice at us after the small reception in the church basement.

I had just completed the last required "education course" that would allow me to teach high school English and had quickly been hired by an elite high school in one of the north-shore suburbs of Chicago. We rented an apartment in Rogers Park, about half-way between our daily commutes, and we began our separate days—he still a student, now in law school; me, paying all the household bills with a job that I both feared and detested.

Since high school had not been a happy time for me, I did not want to teach in one. But with just the master's degree, I could not teach college English, as I had hoped. I had turned down a full ride at Brown University so that I could get a quickie degree to support Luke in order to keep him out of the Vietnam draft. So for two years, I taught wealthy students— some just five years younger than I—and, in my eyes, failed miserably. I had loved college so much and had done so well that it was hard to admit that I knew not the first thing about how to be a good teacher. Afraid and unaccustomed to speaking extemporaneously, I meticulously wrote out my lesson plans, word-for-word.

One day my freshman English class acted up to the point that I had absolutely no control over them. That night I wrote out a reprimand and the next day, hands shaking, I read it to them. "God—she's READING it" shouted out one student. If they had had any respect for me before that, they had none after!

My fellow English teachers and I sat in a huge office behind our separate desks. The lovely, older woman who sat in front of me took pity on me and said that it would be "several years" before I began to think more about the students than about myself. She was right.

I developed upper back pain that became so disabling that I had to lie down between my classes. A student began to stalk me when he did not receive the "A" he had not deserved. I had to have my wisdom teeth removed. I was sick many days with mysterious viruses and had to find my own substitute teachers. And when I came home from work, having driven thirty minutes on the freeway, I was expected to make dinner from the set of "Luke's favorites" that his mother had given me as a wedding present, wash the dishes, and do housework. Because I was making all the money, and perhaps because I was a little bit angry at the whole set-up, I held onto the purse strings too tightly. Now living in completely different worlds, Luke and I did not have the slightest idea of how to talk with each other anymore, still living, as we were, under the threat of his imminent draft. Like most men born in that time, he had not been taught to do any household chores. His mother had handled it all—teaching, housework, children. And I was expected to do the same, with a closed mouth and a smile on my face.

Though I was a married woman and carried all the expectations of that role from the 1950s, I was still essentially a "maiden" for I was emotionally immature, desperately unhappy, and had no one to talk with about my rage and my guilt and my sexual naiveté, certainly not my new husband! The summer before he graduated from law school, Luke was invited to "intern" at a law firm in Denver, CO. He would then join the firm the following fall, assuming that he wasn't drafted first. Even though Luke had drawn a fairly "high" (late-to-be-called) number for the draft lottery, we never knew what might happen or what the government might decide to change with little notice.

Happy as I was to resign my teaching job after two years, that summer I was alone in a hot, tiny apartment in Denver for three months with nothing to do. I knew no one. At the few law firm events that included wives, the senior lawyers patted me on the ass and in other ways patronized me. I started to have what I now realize were panic attacks during the day and laid all my frustration and unhappiness on Luke when he arrived home at night. I wrote in my journal, "what happens when one realizes he [sic] is a failure (by his [sic] standards) at age 25? I have failed as a teacher (for the record). I have lost all self-confidence. From a life of jumping from success to success, laurel to laurel, I have dropped off the edge at age 25, having staked all on the reactions of 200 children. Why am I alive? What is important? To be a success or to be a good person—aware, open, creative, compassionate, involved? I can't write poetry anymore, although I have taught and analyzed its techniques and meanings for two years. Will I be pregnant in a year? Will I be a mother? Will I be a good parent? Is my life over? What will I fill the next 45-50 years with? What will I create? Will I ever succeed? Is it wrong to have such high goals that I will necessarily fail?" I blamed myself, but a part of me knew that the balance of power had shifted between Luke and me. Outside of the college classroom in which we had met, we were no longer equal.

I asked—demanded, really—that he consider an alternate option for the fall. When a draft-deferrable assistant US Attorney position opened in Milwaukee, WI, I begged him to apply for it. When he did, he was hired. I concurrently applied to the Ph.D. program in English at the University of Wisconsin-Milwaukee for the following spring semester, and was accepted.

* * *

The prospect of becoming a student again improved my mood immeasurably, for I knew how to succeed as a student, which had become an important part of my identity. Yet in the meantime I was failing miserably as a wife, was alternately belligerent and passive-aggressive regarding the particulars of that role (making sloppy meals, not wiping the stove for months, and refusing to sew on Luke's missing shirt buttons). There was almost no communication going on between us. I dreamt that I was "a faceless, featureless paper-doll sheen of a mirror, reflecting nothing, aping my terrified movements to run away from myself."

We moved to Milwaukee in late summer of 1970. Luke began work immediately, but I had a semester to kill before I started school in spring of '71. I had little to do but stay "home" in the small suburban apartment rented for us by a colleague at the US Attorney's office. I watched TV and of course heard about all the student protests happening at UW-Milwaukee, as well as at the University of Madison and elsewhere across the nation. The attack on Kent State college students protesting the war by US National Guardsmen had happened in the spring of '70. There was a national student strike in late April and early May of that spring.

On May 6, over 3,000 protesters, including speakers from Students for a Democratic Society, union leaders, activist groups and professors, gathered in front of Mitchell Hall at UW-Milwaukee for a rally and strike action. Then the crowd moved to block access to the Union and occupied the library and the university power plant. The next day strike activities continued with large rallies, cancellation of classes and occupation of various campus buildings. The Chancellor declared a state of emergency on the UWM campus. Over the next week, the library and student union were closed, and, according to the UWM online archives, the Schools of Education and Letters and Science announced their "support for the strikers," indicating that "striking students will not be punished for their participation." However, in the fall of that year, four professors, including two English professors, were

29

tried before a UW System faculty counsel for dismissal for disruptive behavior. The decision provoked student outcry and walkouts, including a 400-person rally in support of the faculty members. Three of the four faculty members, including the two English faculty, were found guilty and formally reprimanded.

This was the climate in which I began my coursework for a doctoral degree in Nineteenth Century American Literature at UW-Milwaukee just a few months later. I had missed all the "action" but enjoyed some of the benefits in the years that followed. Although I was not offered a teaching assistantship until the fall of 1971, when I did begin teaching again, I enjoyed unprecedented freedom in the classroom. College administrators all over the country, including those in Milwaukee, were wary of students, especially graduate students, who had already unionized in Madison in '69 and threatened to at UWM.

Therefore, between 1971 and 1976 when I received my doctorate, in my freshman English classes, I could teach (say) just about anything I wanted to and could give whatever grades I wanted to—usually all A's. I remember sitting cross-legged in bell-bottoms on my desk at the front of the room, braless, smoking, and gesturing expressively as I spoke without podium or notes. What a change from the timid high school teacher of just three years earlier! One clearly surprised male freshman offered, eyes on my bouncing breasts, "Gee, I had no idea college could be like THIS!"

But I'm getting ahead of myself.

In the fall of 1971 I met with a young faculty advisor to select my courses for my first semester. He was not one of the faculty members "reprimanded" for taking part in the student strikes the previous semester, but he was obviously on their side. They were the "stars" of the English department. They taught creative writing and held classes off-campus wherever they wanted to. I was a little afraid of them.

Jamie met with me in his fourth-floor walkup office with dormer windows in an old building that reminded me of those wonderful classes with Benjamin Spencer. But in Jamie's office were soft reading chairs, dirty windows, overflowing ashtrays, and jazz/blues albums scattered everywhere, with Mose Allison or Carly Simon or Buffy St. Marie or James Taylor or Carole King playing on the turntable. He was, in his "spare time," the DJ for the campus night jazz and blues station.

Not conventionally handsome, Jamie was nevertheless quite tall with sideburns and dark, thick, collar-length hair. He had a very low, intensely sexy voice and a corresponding penetrating, though lidded, stare: "bedroom eyes." He strolled into his office smoking, wearing worn blue jeans and suede boots with no socks, his long sleeves rolled up to show his forearms and a thick turquoise bracelet. During my initial session with him, he quickly reviewed my scholastic record, looked up at me with those eyes and then told me in that low voice that I "had potential"; therefore (suddenly all business), I should drop the 19th-century as my focus. The "action"— where it was "at"—was the Present, he said. The writers and philosophers of the early 20th century, such as Edmund Husserl, Andre Gide, Jacques Derrida, Roland Barthes, and Maurice Merleau-Ponty, were driving a new pedagogy of contemporary English programs such as ours, which had recently had the good luck to hire the prestigious "deconstructionist" scholar Ihab Hassan. Jamie suggested that I take some of Hassan's classes as well as other literature and philosophy courses from the 20th century and scrap the seminars on those "has-beens," Whitman, Hawthorne and Dickinson.

At thirty-three, Jamie was only about five years older than I. The youngest English faculty member at UWM ever to receive tenure, he was a protégé of Hassan and taught courses to undergraduates about (again) anything he wanted to. What he wanted to teach were contemporary, controversial books then being written by John Barth, Norman Mailer, John Updike, Saul Bellow, James Baldwin and other male writers "deconstructing" their maleness. He also had a penchant for the Occult, and taught some of Carlos Castaneda's books as well as some of Jane Roberts' "Seth" books, in which she "channeled" the "lessons" of an "oversoul" named Seth.

This was all very heady stuff for me. So I willingly put my love for Emily Dickinson and Walt Whitman to the side and started to read 20th century poets, including Wallace Stevens, about whose use of metaphor I eventually wrote my dissertation. Ihab Hassan directed it, and I received my doctorate in '76 with "high honors."

The arts were finally catching up to the sciences, especially the theoretical physicists of the 1930s such as Einstein, Schrödinger, and others, who had questioned whether there was really an observable, determinable "difference" between an object and its observer—indeed, whether there was any "thing" like a fixed reality. Theologians such as Dietrich Bonhoeffer were questioning the literal aspects of the Christian religion (his *Letters and Papers from Prison* I sent to my bewildered mother in the doomed attempt to open an "adult" conversation about religion). Everything—and I mean everything—was up for grabs.

Obviously, I was enticed by such drastically different literary, scientific, and religious theories than those I had been brought up with. And I was also seduced by the minds of those men (never women) who were at the forefront of such theories. Hassan held "soirées" for a few favored colleagues and graduate students. I was one of only two women who were ever invited. I thought that this showed how "special" I was to be accepted in a man's intellectual world. In 1972 I wrote a "deconstructionist" paper on, yes, Emily Dickinson. Hassan's comment was simply "immensely impressive!" I was so proud of myself, bringing 20th-century sensibilities to one of my favorite 19th-century poets.

* * *

Unfortunately, Jamie was married. Amazingly, I believed him when he said that "only I" could now really "understand" him. The joke about the man saying that his wife "didn't understand him" was not a joke to me. I had never heard it before. I certainly believed that my current husband "didn't understand" me. And so, though Jamie was never my professor, we necked a lot in his office, and wrote long, tortured "deconstructed" love letters to each other, which we surreptitiously left in each other's mail cubicles. It wasn't long before I believed that I was in love despite Jamie's new growing opposition to traditional marriage. "Open marriage," based on the eponymous best-selling book by George and Nena O'Neill, was a concept based on the "sexual revolution" of the 60s, which had touted "free love" and the abandonment of old-style (read "monogamous") marriage.

Luke, of course, was clueless. Instead of talking openly with him, I would come home at night after a day of classes to make underdone meat loaf or overdone chuck roast, obvious passive-aggressive gestures. I was becoming quite angry about the gender roles in our marriage. At one point when he asked me to mend one of his shirts, I shot back, "Why don't you do it yourself?" He was dumbfounded, responding only that I should do it "out of love." Wasn't that what wives did? It was what his mother had done for his father. I was finding my voice, and it was often an angry one. After four years of marriage and Luke's having completed law school with the prospect of good job options lined up, the next step for us would have been children and for me to have stopped working or looking for a permanent academic job. But I balked. Since our marriage, I had used the brand-new high-dose "birth control" pills available in the late 60s. Barbara Seaman's *The Doctor's Case against the Pill*, published in 1969, warned of the risks of blood clots (especially if one smoked, which I still did), heart attack and stroke (which ran in our family), depression (ditto), weight gain, and loss of libido. I went off the pill after about one year, blaming it partly for my anxiety, migraines, and other physical issues; however, it was not until 1988 that the kind of pill I had been taking was banned by the FDA. With very few options remaining, I was fitted for a diaphragm, which I used with spermicide every single time. This method served me for the rest of my child-bearing years, except for those times when I actively sought to become pregnant.

My parents suspected that something was wrong. That year, my mother sent me an article from *The Wichita Eagle* called "Wife Controls Climate of Home." In it, a "life specialist" from Kansas State University wrote, "A woman must work on her own emotional behavior. It takes real effort to be thoughtful, enthusiastic, affectionate, and understanding. It takes almost no effort to be dogmatic, cranky, irritable, and depressed," she adds. "The wife's disposition does have a great deal to do with her husband's attitude toward himself." Reading this now, I believe that my mother had tried during her entire marriage to be these things for my father. It could be one reason why she always considered herself to be a "failure."

In 1972, Luke and I headed off to a marriage counselor, but by then I knew I wasn't fully invested in being restored to a conventional marriage, and I saw no way of transforming it. I was falling in love with someone else.

In the middle of a January day in 1973, I returned to Luke's and my flat, packed just a few things, and left in what can only be described as a cowardly way, by putting a cursory note on the kitchen table. Luke and I did meet several times after that to talk, but I was adamant about not coming back. Luke was always a kind man and didn't deserve the hurt and humiliation caused by what I had done. Eventually, he recovered, however, and married a much better wife than I— one of his legal secretaries—and moved to Seattle where he became a very successful lawyer who defended "white collar" crime. We were always friends, and still are. About ten years ago, when he was visiting Milwaukee, I finally apologized in person for the cowardly way in which I had left so many years ago, and he accepted my apology. We both agreed that given the turbulent times, our youth and inexperience in relationships, our marriage hadn't had much chance for success.

Meanwhile, Jamie and I took a large studio apartment with a tiny kitchen and bathroom, far from campus. Even so, the English department pretended to be scandalized (not that there weren't already many affairs going on between professors, advisors, and students). We quickly set up a small household, the upkeep of which was carefully gender-neutral. We both made "Hungry Man Dinners" in the microwave; he vacuumed; I changed the sheets and did the laundry. I also probably scrubbed the kitchen sink and bathtub, because no man I've ever known has even thought of it. We filed our respective spouses for divorce.

"Our song" became the 1965 hit by Buffy Sainte-Marie: "Until It's Time for You to Go". The germane lines turned out to be these:

Take my hand
We'll make a space
In the lives that we planned
And here we'll stay
Until it's time for you to go

Don't ask why
Don't ask how
Don't ask for ever, honey
Love me, now
I'll never in my life see you again
Still I'll stay
Until it's time for you to go

Another of "our songs," which came out in 1971, and which, like Buffy's, we played over and over on Jamie's expensive turntable and speakers, was Carly Simon's "Anticipation" in which the disturbing lines for me were these:

And tomorrow we might not be together
I'm no prophet and I don't know nature's ways
So I'll try and see into your eyes right now
And stay right here 'cause these are the good old days

Looking back, it's so obvious that the romantic *zeitgeist* was not about permanence or stability. A war was on; the civil rights and women's movements were leading to unknowns; the time would come when Jamie would inevitably leave me and our young child for yet another "adventure." But in 1971, compellingly, these lyrics spoke to me of release from stagnation and dead ends: of flow, of my being "chosen," of living in the amazing present, damn the consequences. And it was glorious.

We spent a lot of time in bed, which was a revelation to me. Women's sexuality was "coming out of the closet." In 1970, the Boston Women's Health Book Collective published a 193-page course booklet on stapled newsprint, selling for 75 cents, entitled "Women and Their Bodies"—revolutionary for its open discussion of women's sexuality. Republished in 1971 by New England Free Press for 40 cents, and then picked up by Simon & Schuster in 1973, the book, retitled *Our Bodies, Ourselves*, came out just in time for our relationship. In part of the Preface, the eleven women authors collectively write,

> *Picture a woman trying to do work and to enter into equal and satisfying relationships with other people when she feels physically weak because she has never tried to be strong; when she drains her energy trying to change her face, her figure, her hair, her smells, to match some ideal norm set by magazines, movies and TV, when she feels confused and ashamed of the menstrual blood that every month appears from some dark place in her body; when her internal body processes are a mystery to her and surface only to cause her trouble (an unplanned pregnancy or cervical cancer); when she does not*

understand or enjoy sex and concentrates her sexual drives into aimless romantic fantasies, perverting and misusing a potential energy because she has been brought up to deny it. Learning to understand, accept, and be responsible for our physical selves, we are freed of some of these preoccupations and can start to use our untapped energies. Our image of ourselves is on a firmer base, we can be better friends and better lovers, better people, more self-confident, more autonomous, stronger and more whole.

Well, that certainly described me in 1973. My mother had never talked to me about sex, except to describe the "rags" she used to have to wash by hand during "that time of the month." We were so lucky to have Kotex, she said. Tampax made women "sick" and I was not to use them. She did monitor whether, at night, my hands were on top of the covers (which they often were not). Touching oneself "down there" was something called "homosexuality" which was forbidden by the Bible and punished by going to hell. I don't think I *actually* believed any of that, but her attitudes nevertheless made me think of my body and its sensations as a guilty mystery. My girlfriends never talked about "it" either.

Therefore, I don't think I was ever as aware of the cultural revolution going on around me as I was bowled over by this new sexual relationship and what my body was capable of. As constantly as we made love, Jamie and I also talked incessantly about "deconstruction" and how it applied to our relationship; we read ourselves into the characters of Carlos Castaneda's books, seeking true "Power" (in a male sense; the female shamans were portrayed as pretty deadly) as opposed to the "false power" of "society."

The honeymoon was not to last. In August of that year (1973) I write, "Jamie is at the psychiatrist this afternoon— for the first time in four or five months. I am afraid, myself, of slipping into depression. I have many of the symptoms, even though my doctor says they are signs of physical and mental exhaustion. I *am* exhausted. Jamie has threatened suicide, and at one point I didn't know whether or not I would ever see him alive again." Feeling overwhelmed by his needs and emotions, I started taking some time to myself.

I visited my friend and fellow student, Mark, one day when Jamie was off somewhere, threatening suicide. Mark, an ex-priest, ten years older than I, was making a cake in the oven. I remember asking him, "How can you make cake when someone is threatening suicide?" He replied, looking at me steadily, "That's exactly what you do." It took me a long time to understand that, as well as his comment when I talked about the importance of "Risk." He said that there was a difference between "risk" and "foolhardiness," and gave the example of diving into a body of water without knowing how deep it is. Good advice, but I only partly understood what he was telling me, and still felt committed to the relationship with Jamie who, ultimately, never even came close to commitment (though we were married in jeans before a judge in August of '74) or, for that matter, to committing suicide.

Four:

"Highly Sensitive People" Fooling Around in the Halls of Academia

A side from talking with my fellow-student Mark, the ex-priest, I took long drives alone in the countryside. I took a few airplane glider lessons (I had always wanted to fly like my dad). One day, still disturbed by Jamie's mental condition, I drove to Lizard Mound, a prehistoric Indian burial site near West Bend, WI. I wrote, "The woods were very green and thick. The flies were bad, but they kept me moving. I knew I had to walk the whole path, neither hurrying nor tarrying, meeting my Fear, and that perhaps something would be there for me at the end—at the mound in the shape of a giant bird. When I reached the Bird Mound, I felt a Presence there. As I stepped up on the mound, thoughts started to occur: I must walk each segment slowly; I must not step off until I was finished, that it would be 'nice' to find even a small feather on that particular mound, that if I didn't it would be a sign that I was on the 'wrong path'—generally—in life. I walked the bird's body, returned, walked the right wing, returned, started to walk the left wing, heard a rustle high in the tree above me, looked up, saw nothing, looked down, and saw a huge eagle feather at my feet. I felt awe, power, humility, and wonder. I finished the walk on the left wing, returned to the center, gave thanks, and left."

It turned out to be a hawk or seagull feather, but still. It was definitely a numinous experience. "Numin"—the Latin—means "divine power." The word "numinous" also comes from *numen*, meaning the spiritual characteristic of a thing or place. A numinous experience is said also to have a very personal quality, in that a person feels to be in the presence of a wholly "Other." The term has been used in many contexts: Carl Jung got the term from Rudolf Otto's book *The Idea of the Holy.* According to Sarah N. Aron, Ph.D., author of *The Highly Sensitive Person: How to Thrive When the World Overwhelms You* (2012):

> *A central tenet of Jungian psychology is that the numinous heals us. The numinous was Carl Jung's real interest, from boyhood—not studying or treating mental illness. But fortunately for all of us, it turned out that the numinous does seem to heal mental illness, as shamans and other healers have always known. Thus Jungians look for and find the numinous in dreams, in waking visions and "active imagination," in the numinous aspects of therapy relationships and other relationships outside of therapy, in spontaneous artistic productions, and in meaningful coincidences or synchronistic events, which become unusually common while engaged in deep inner work. (Synchronicities are events that are connected for a reason, but not by the usual physical causes—for example, you dream about a turtle and the next day you see a turtle for the first time in years, then hear a song about a turtle, and have someone call you a turtle because*

*of your hard shell.) Jungians will interpret this material,
finding it symbolic of something personal (maybe, "you
spend a lot of time in your shell"), but also symbolic of an
aspect of the numinous itself (for example, in some
creation myths, the universe is carried by the turtle).
Finding a personal link to the numinous is often
exceedingly meaningful and healing in itself, for many
reasons you can imagine. It is part of why HSPs do well
in, and like so much, Jungian psychotherapy.*

Aron's research suggests that between 15-20% of the
population can be termed "highly sensitive": i.e. easily
overwhelmed by external stimuli; prefer to avoid violent
movies; need to withdraw from stress by retreating for privacy
and relief; avoid upsetting situations; have rich and complex
inner lives and high "emotional reactivity." Quoting her work
in the recent book *Wired to Create: Unraveling the Mysteries
of the Creative Mind* (2016), Kaufman and Gregoire note that
"High levels of sensitivity are correlated with not only
creativity but also overlapping traits such as spirituality,
intuition, mystical experiences, and connection to art and
nature." In 1973, there was no positive term for this group of
people, except perhaps "spaced out," and I'm sure that's how
Jamie and I seemed to many people, including our families.
Jamie dropped acid a few times, but I did not, sensing that it
would overwhelm me. Another current term for what Jamie
and I were doing is exhibiting "apophenia"—the human
tendency to see patterns in unexpected places—which can
describe anyone from artists to schizophrenics. Recent
research suggests that this tendency exists on a spectrum for
all human beings, with "highly sensitive persons" being some
of the most persistent "meaning-makers" of all. As a child,
sitting on the toilet with intense cramps from IBS (Irritable
Bowel Syndrome—another syndrome not fully explained
until modern times), I would distract myself from the pain by
seeing faces and telling stories about the figures I "saw" in the
linoleum on our bathroom floor.

In any case, Jamie and I were two "highly sensitive people" making life miserable for each other. When I broke down in my doctor's office, he suggested that Jamie and I—two neurotic depressives, as he put it—fed on each other, dragging each other down. One can't change people, he said, only situations. That if I would stay, he went on, I would need to be a 'stone pillar,' whereas that was exactly what I needed. Coming on to me a little, he added that I was a "real woman" who needed a "real man"—i.e. "a fist in a velvet glove." Like many doctors treating women in those days, he gave me tranquilizers and sleeping pills.

I started feeling drugged most of the time, as if I were trying to move through water. My father had written to me, chastising me for breaking up my marriage, suggesting that I only wanted what I thought would bring me pleasure, not what was "right." The only excuse he could accept for my leaving Luke was the possibility that Luke had beaten me. When I disabused him of that notion, he blamed me even more, even as he still offered to help. And when I refused his "help"— knowing that it would make me ever more dependent upon and indebted to him— he considered me even more selfish and stubborn, citing my mother's recurrent illnesses as my fault. She constantly sent me religious books and letters wondering "where she went wrong with me."

My father used to tell me the story of a man whose car had a flat tire at night in the countryside. Apparently, the man had no jack to change the tire, so he started up a long drive to a farmhouse. While he was walking, he kept thinking about what the farmer would say: that he was angry about being wakened in the middle of the night; that he would probably be concerned that a stranger was at his door; that even if he had a jack, which he probably didn't, he no doubt would not let him borrow it to fix his car. By the time the man reached the farmhouse, he was quite angry, so when the farmer did indeed answer the door, the man shouted, "You can just keep your damn jack!" and walked away.

Apparently, my father thought that I was like the man with the flat tire. Maybe so. A part of me, perhaps like a part of him, didn't believe that I deserved help. Nor did I want my father to retain his power over me. Late in his life, referring to the fact that as a child I was called "Little Lauren" because our stubborn temperaments were similar, he gave me this advice, not looking me in the eye: "Don't ever do things just to make someone like you. Sometimes they don't like themselves." I interpreted this to mean that my father had never really liked himself: a rail-thin chain smoker all of his life, his chronic anxiety and obsession with electronics had made him virtually inaccessible to his family.

Nevertheless, both he and my mother had shared what I would call numinous moments with me. My mother told me, when I was in my teens, that the night after my sister had died, my mother was tormenting herself with what Marilyn might be going through: alone, afraid, not knowing what had happened or where she was. She said she felt like she was going "wild" with grief when she heard a voice saying clearly and calmly, "Marilyn is all right." At that, she said, she calmed down immediately. As a teen, I scoffed at this, as did my father. But I never forgot it. That moment did not "cure" her grief, but I'm sure it was a solace when she remembered it.

Similarly, late in his life, my father told me this story. When he was a teen, he and his brothers shot coyotes and jackrabbits (considered "vermin" to farmers), not only for the bounty, but for "fun." One day, he said, when he went to retrieve the rabbit he had just shot, he experienced a great enveloping sadness at the death of that limp, warm creature that had just moments before been alive. Since then, he told me, he never killed another living thing just "for fun."

I suspect that such moments occur to many people, often at times of great emotion, but also sometimes just out of the blue.

In any case, in the mid-1970s, despite all of our personal drama that distressed my parents so much, Jamie and I were still teaching. I had finished the coursework for my dissertation on Wallace Stevens and was teaching courses like "Inner Worlds and Visions" and "The Self and the Other" as a lecturer: courses that had originally been designed by Jamie. Surprisingly, more than thirty years later, in 2009, while teaching freshman composition in the adult-education department of Marquette University, I received this email from one of the other teachers there, who was, amazingly, one of my former students at UWM:

> *If I am pressed to identify a single course in my educational background that changed my life, it was "Inner Worlds and Visions." I can't tell you how often I have spoken about that course. Just last summer my wife and I were riding bicycles past that hall where you taught and we stopped in the circle. I looked up at the window and told the story again.*
>
> *I always recall the dozen books (all of which are still in my library -Siddhartha, John Lily et. al.) and the dialectic of fear and curiosity that you chartered in me; the fear that let me know something important was about [to happen] and the curiosity that led me through the fear. I remember how difficult the readings were; so much so that I actually cut the class, sitting in front of the building trying to force myself to join in the discussions. Fear won that day but eventually I did!*
>
> *You were the beginning of a lifelong acquaintance with my inner self that culminated recently in a decision to prepare for the second half of life with a master's degree where I wrote on Self-Leadership and Career Decisions. I can only say thank you - and offer the possibility that your work may perhaps again impact someone else's life - through mine. I can only hope!*
>
> *Most of all I treasure the memory of how you introduced the final exam with a simple request: "When you finish, turn it in, and leave alone but not lonely."*

Sometimes, when I look back upon the personal craziness of that time, it's hard to realize that Jamie and I were both good, (mostly) professional and effective teachers, who touched a lot of lives. The only difference was that he was a tenured Associate Professor, and I was an ABD (All But Dissertation), who could teach only at the pleasure of the English Department that would eventually award my degree. After that, I would have to get a "real job."

By fall of 1973, I was officially diagnosed with depression. Obviously, I was, in some sense, still a child, still a maiden, dependent on others for my sense of well-being, of self-worth, longing for the same security that I outwardly disdained. I was 28 years old and at the start of the astrological "Saturn return" (the return of Saturn to the place where it was when one was born) which occurs to everyone about that age. Western astrologers believe it to be a time of transition, when one hopefully leaves behind childhood and takes on the perspective and responsibilities of adulthood.

Through one means or another, Jamie and I were also exploring the "mysteries" of astrology, Tarot, and the *I Ching* . We had our charts done and interpreted by a friend of his. To this day, I occasionally use these tools to understand what might be going on in my life at a certain time in order to give me a larger understanding of how to deal with it. The down side of such tools is that one can easily use them for more unhealthy purposes: e.g., to "predict" the future in order to have more control over what seems to be an uncontrollable life. Now, in my 70s, I use these tools sparingly, and only to give me additional perspective on what is happening in my life. In my 20s, during my first Saturn return, I used them to try to reassure myself that what I wanted to happen would indeed eventually happen.

Jamie, like Luke, was a Cancer (their birthdays were only six days apart, though in different years); I am a Pisces. Both are water signs (as is Scorpio—the birth sign of my third husband, Ben), which rule the emotions, dreams, nurturing, the arts, and receptivity. On the flip side, people whose sun

45

signs are in water can have a tendency to brood, a susceptibility to mood swings, and can become self-indulgent, controlling, and hostage to a fantasy world. Reading about these things gave me a new sense of validation: an understanding of myself and my romantic partners that I did not have before, but it did not necessarily make dealing with everything easier.

It turned out that the mood "pills" I was taking were much too strong: my new doctor—a psychiatrist—said they were given mainly to violent patients on mental wards. Instead, he prescribed a mild tranquilizer and Elavil before bedtime. Unlike my previous doctor, he said I was NOT manic-depressive, just "cyclic" in my highs and lows. After Jamie's father's death, and after some Tarot readings by a woman he knew, he cut off all relations with his mother, believing her to be a witch. I was apparently NOT a witch—not an evil one anyway—merely a "power woman," though later in my life I did consider myself to be Wiccan, in the most positive sense of "witchcraft." Whenever I tried to pull away from Jamie's vision of things, he accused me of completely "abandoning" him, of negating our "togetherness," whereas I was, I believe, simply trying to develop a healthy adult self apart from him, in addition to my own authentic voice, so that I could relate to him in a better way.

Ultimately, he left me for another graduate student in 1978 when our daughter, Julie, was almost a year old.

Adhesions

You are still bound to me by adhesions, scar tissue
tethering us together, tentacles hooking into my organs,
     stretching

them tight. Four abdominal incisions leave outer scars shiny
and smooth, the inner a web of tangled yarn darning over the
     egg of empty

space. The gut's a second brain sprung from the same cells; it
loops, ducks under and around the claws of fiber reaching out
     to grasp,

limit movement, tie it down. The scalpel is only a partial cure.
Like the deep roots of weeds they grow back. You are long

gone but my irritable bowel apparently remembers your name
and pinches if I think of when you were in my life and I in
     yours.

Why couldn't you have blasted me through the heart? Gut-
shot one lingers, tries to hold back one's separate life

with hands come to seem like leaky lids. Did Eve escape
Adam's tight rib cage to leave adhesions in his sleeping

heart? More likely, motherless Eve was the one slit
open, from *her* tugged lover, children, womb, time:

pried open, only to be basted closed, while inside
pale as pearl, what looks like healing is just the beginning of
     pain.

Five:

Selling My Dulcimer (The Queen of Cups) on eBay

I sold my dulcimer today, in 2017, on eBay—the one that was hand-made for me at an Indiana writer's conference in 1978, while Jamie, my second husband, was "baby-sitting" our daughter while sleeping with his eventual third wife, Jill. It (the dulcimer) was signed, "To the Queen of Cups."

The only person seriously interested in my dulcimer on eBay indicated that, given the picture and description I had provided, his offer of $100 was reasonable, considering its age. I responded by saying that I would email him a story about how I got the dulcimer. If, after he read the story, he gave me his Very Best Offer, I would accept it.

Here is the story: In June of 1978, my second husband, our one-year-old daughter, and I went to a conference called "The Great Mother and the New Father" featuring the poet

Robert Bly. We stayed in a cabin where there was a fireplace, and I started to write in my journal about fire: "There must be space between the logs in order for the air to feed the fire. One separates in order to transform. One can never write directly about a thing. One must attend to the moment, trusting that in attention is the essence of what is to be articulated. What is combustion? When things come together, something breaks open. It is wood's nature to burn. One simply arranges components in a certain manner and wood burns—fire occurs—naturally, out of itself." Clearly, I was writing hopefully, in metaphor, about our marriage. I still did not trust writing or talking "directly about a thing."

Still at the conference, I meet "Lou," also a Pisces, who gave me a head massage, having no experience but being willing to give it his complete attention. That complete attention—commitment, but not to directions, structure, or ideal—is very close to love, no matter its duration.

Bly gave a lecture about the Great Mother. I sat in the back, outside, alone with Julie, who was softly babbling to herself. Bly turned to me and said that she was disturbing him and asked me to leave. I was incensed, and later told him that in so many words: how could he purport to be a disciple of the Great Mother and yet ask a mother and child to leave HIS LECTURE? He nodded, smiled, and dismissed me: "I thought you'd be upset," he said.

Despite Bly's being a jerk, I enjoyed myself at the conference. I liked the sense of being in a group of people who shared more or less the same values, but with whom I need not have an ongoing relationship: Bessie, the midwife and singer, mother of Kerrie; Rusty, with whom I danced in the sun; Lou, who gave me the head massage and taught me something about Platonic love; Connie, coming from suburbia; Gay, pregnant with her fourth child; Warren with his banjo; Jason, with his cardiology practice in Denver; Radha with her bare breasts, red hair, and calm hands; Connie with her poem, courage, strength, beauty and youth. I probably had some small exchange with each of the 100 people there. Jamie was apparently occupied elsewhere, not interested in such activities. The three of us returned to Milwaukee: Jamie and Julie had mild colds, but I felt whole, healed, at one, and at peace.

A few days later, on June 14, ten years after I was married to my first husband, Jamie took a new apartment, away from us. His words when he left were "I love you. Don't forget me," which, of course, made it seem as if he were going even farther away.

For a while I didn't even realize that his leaving was, indeed, permanent. I had spiritual guides, such as the Tarot, and friends. A baby and a dog. Parents. I had $3000, all that I needed at the time. I offered to lead an informal workshop on journal writing at the Indiana Writers' Conference I was going to soon. I bought new tires for Crazy Horse (our red VW bug).

The garden became all my own doing. In fact, I realized that nearly everything in our apartment *had* been *my doing,* once Jamie took away his books, records, and paintings.

The next day, June 15, I write, "Ten years ago tonight I was freshly married for the first time. Now, it is 8:00, just turning dusk. I have finished mowing the lawn, which I started two days ago. I am sweating under my breasts. Thin wet moons appear on my orange t-shirt. It is also dirty from carrying the snow tires up to the attic. Quite a change from the blindingly-white wedding dress and yellow going-away suit. The wedding pictures are still upstairs in the attic somewhere.

"Tonight there is no question of whether Jamie is coming home. He's not. That started to sink in sometime this afternoon as Julie grew progressively crankier and I knew there would be no relief. I am tired. I am the center of the world for a neurotic dog and a growing baby. I have half a lover from whom I receive half his love."

Jamie had moved out so that he could actively pursue his relationship with another female graduate student, Jill. He believed that he could carry on as my husband and Julie's father even though half of his time would be spent with another woman and another half with his other children by his first marriage. Wait: that's three halves.

Weary, no longer really surprised at what had happened, I nevertheless felt mostly positive about my ability to "cope" with my child and responsibilities. I went to Summerfest, for the first time alone with just Julie, and we got caught in the rain, but we had a great time together. What I missed most was talking with Jamie—having a sounding board for my ideas. When he came over, we made love occasionally, but there was no real intimacy.

An immediate change was that I had to look for part-time child care. A retired nurse, the mother of a friend, agreed to do this, and she proved to be an affordable godsend. At that point I still believed that Jamie just needed "time away" in order to "find himself." He was concerned about his own aging and his stalled career (at associate professor). I had forgotten all about the lines from "our songs" like the one by Carly Simon: *We'll make a space/In the lives that we planned/And here we'll stay/Until it's time for you to go.* Well, the time had apparently come for him to go.

But we were *married*, and somehow, in 1978, I still thought of that as a guarantee that he would come back even as I knew that I had not returned to Luke. I had forgotten about the down-side of that once-seductive word, "risk." That was the word with which Jamie had seduced me in 1973. Yes, yes, he was married with four young children, but both he and his wife had had previous affairs, no big deal. He was involved in the spirit of the times which encouraged things like risk, exploration, freedom from old structures. So one day he simply asked me to come away with him. We were sitting in a park and he pointed to a line of trees to the south: "We don't know what's beyond, right now," he said, "but if we are willing to risk everything, we will find out together and experience things beyond our wildest imaginations." Intoxicating stuff. Hard to resist.

We had five years before I apparently grew stale to him. Once a mother, I was no longer the "risk taker" I had been.

Little did he know what big risks mothers really take. Now, alone, I found that I had time to think thoughts and feel feelings through by myself without having them resolved or cut off by discussion and exchange. I read Liv Ullman's *Changing*, a memoir about her relationship with Ingmar Bergman (the Swedish filmmaker), their daughter, and her acting career. She speaks of the love for her work, the relative unimportance of success. Yet she is honest about the benefits of financial security. She feels guilty about time spent away from her daughter. She thinks about why her relationships with men have ended. The relationship with Bergman came to an end, she says, because they had become too isolated, clutching, 'secure.'

All of these insights I had had myself. Yet I did crave security for both me and Julie. Having a child had grounded me in a way I had never been before. But I wondered whether I was "unlovable" and felt in some way "unworthy" of love— at least of loving with a "light hand" that has no need for permanence. This still does not come easily or naturally to me.

I gathered materials for a journal workshop I had offered to hold at the Indiana Writers' Conference: the journals and diaries of May Sarton, Henry Bugbee, Virginia Woolf, Anaïs Nin. The keynote speakers at the week-long conference were May Swenson, Ursula LeGuin, and David Ignatow, all of whom I admired. Jamie agreed to "baby-sit" for Julie, laughing and calling me a 'pious bitch' the night before I left, probably in response to some snarky comment I had made.

The temperature in Indiana was a humid 100 degrees, and I was staying on the eighth floor of a college dormitory without air conditioning. However, the air-conditioned library there had a collection of Sylvia Plath's manuscripts, still owned by Ted Hughes, her husband. I could request what I wanted to see, so I chose three drafts of her poem "The Moon and the Yew Tree." I had to fill out forms, sit in a special room, and check my bags outside. And even then, what came were mere Xeroxes. Nevertheless, I felt it to be worthwhile, as a poet, to see the progression of her drafts—what she omitted and what she had changed.

But most of the week I found myself irritable, and compared that irritability to Jung's theory about a woman's animus, which I imagined as a dwarf. For Jung, the "animus" was a symbol of the masculine qualities of a woman's subconscious, which need to be integrated into consciousness in order to achieve "wholeness," just as a man's "anima" contains his unconscious feminine qualities. These are generally positive processes; however, in a culture where the male elements of rationality and intelligence are discouraged in women, then these qualities may be seen as irritability, aggressiveness, argumentativeness, destructiveness, and insensitivity.

However sexist that way of looking at things might seem today, I believed, like Plath, that I was under the thumb of an un-integrated animus. I wrote, "The dwarf clings to clarity. Like everything else, however, clarity cannot be clung to. When one has used a raft to cross a river, one leaves it on the other side. To carry it onward is to be encumbered. Thus the dwarf must give up clarity to cut something new out of the cloth of consciousness. The pattern is always changing.

"Yesterday's key does not fit today's lock. The dwarf thinks his skeleton key will unlock everything, but he is wrong. He needs to become a smith: to forge his own keys (and sometimes his own locks). He needs to become interested in the forging process. He needs to forge the river. Thus Sylvia's dwarf saw her through drafts of creation. But in the end it was the old dwarf who won out: an un-tempered father, he ultimately killed her." Again, I was using a metaphor to separate my "fate" from Plath's deadly response to *her* cheating husband and *her* burden of single motherhood.

No one at the conference seemed interested in journal writing. No one signed up for my free workshop.

One of the perks that came with my payment for the conference, however, was a meeting with a "real" poet to discuss my work. The woman, probably a graduate student, told me my poetry was well-written but too mythological for her taste. It was not "grounded." There was no sense of individuality in it, and the punctuation was not consistent. I admit that these things were probably true in the poems that she saw. She also told me something more valuable: that on the night before she was divorced, she kept thinking of lines of her own poems. She knew that they were *hers*—that they were things she owned that could not be taken away or lost.

This reminded me of something I had done the day after Jamie first left. Leaving Julie with my friend's mother, I took myself into a secluded park by the river and hunkered down under the foliage where no one could see me. As I cried, I told myself that I was the same person I had always been and that I would always have that same self, no matter what happened. Slowly, I was learning to mother myself, as well as my child. Many decades later, I found that same technique useful as I read John Bradshaw's famous book *Homecoming: Reclaiming and Healing Your Inner Child (1992)*.

At the conference, there were talks by an agent and by an editor from Knopf. They were young, thin, expensively dressed, and aloof. They were making money, and they were "making it" at a young age by marketing literature. They dealt with it as a commodity, something that Lewis Hyde, in his later book *The Gift (1983)*, found to be the root cause of why many artists and writers in our country cannot make a living at their craft.

I met with May Swenson, who told me simply to write *more*—the best advice I've ever received. I had dinner with a woman in her fifties who had just published a novel. She had also raised four children. Coincidentally, she also had gone to Ohio Wesleyan University and knew my beloved professor Ben Spencer. She advised me to set aside two hours a week just to mail out my work to publishers. I met another woman who lived in a trailer in the forests of Oregon with another woman and her two sons. She wrote fantasy novels, raised German Shepherds, and worked in Portland two days a week to support the rest of her life. It sounded like a good plan to me.

On the third day of the conference I saw a poster offering locally hand-made dulcimers. I met with the instrument maker and ordered one to my liking: identifying my best self with the Tarot's Queen of Cups, I asked that a chalice be carved into the fret. Traditionally, the  Queen of Cups represents a woman in her maturity who has the most positive characteristics of the water signs: she is compassionate, intuitive, and emotionally stable. Vicki Noble's card (above) created for her *Motherpeace* deck (1981)—which I still use—describes her as the archetypal Muse: "she can swim through the deep waters of the unconscious like a fish, and she can breathe air into her lungs and engage in human thought." She inspires poetry and, in the image, holds a lyre, one of the oldest stringed instruments in the world: "The sounds made by the Priestess of Cups are heard by the whale who circles below her, communing with her on psychic and musical levels. She represents the Soul—the inner part of the being, which mediates between the spirit world and daily events."

When my dulcimer was finished and I held it across my lap, I was amazed at its beauty. I could not really afford $100 of my meager lecturer's salary, but the instrument confirmed my vision of who I was, which was worth any price at the time. I wanted to learn to play music again, in a different way. I thought that, perhaps, it would connect with my poetry, but that didn't really matter.

I attended readings by both Ursula LeGuin and David Ignatow. I enjoyed both, but was stung when, after I asked LeGuin about the influence of Taoism on her work, she snapped that she "never discussed that." I felt foolish and clumsy. I sat down in the woods, my go-to refuge to try to calm myself and deal, once again, with my feeling of being rejected.

When I returned home, it was good to see Julie, but Jamie told me, with no sense that I would be upset, that he and his new lover, Jill, had slept in what was then "my" bed with Julie lying in her crib at the foot. I felt as though I had been punched in the stomach. Still believing, incredible as it now seems, that we had some kind of a future together, an "open marriage," I demanded that he at least have a vasectomy. He agreed, though Jill was furious that I would ask such a thing. Too bad, I thought to myself.

I brought back toys for Julie, and she especially seemed to like the toy xylophone. She was growing so fast—was so alert. She pulled herself up to stand and then wanted to do it all the time.

Last year's garden was over-run with weeds. I felt angry, hurt, anxious, and alone. On the Fourth of July weekend, it grew dark, and families all along the block made their noise. A few days later tears came in the parking lot of the grocery store as I saw a 'family'—a man with one arm around a pregnant woman, the other holding a child's hand. What I felt then was indeed envy.

There were only two tropical fish left in Jamie's disease-ravaged tank—a bottom-feeder and the beautiful Beta I had bought. They seemed lonely too, but nevertheless responsive and apparently hungry. Apparently, I thought, life, with all its appetites, goes on.

Jamie's 38th birthday came and went that summer. He told me excitedly about his 'vision' that everyone in his 'network' have their own place but come to live with *him* periodically. Sometimes he would live with *Jill*—his new lover—sometimes with me; perhaps sometimes with one of his male friends. I was crying as he left, so full of his new 'vision,' moving away from me for his own 'fulfillment.' I went for a walk with Julie. We saw a litter of new puppies. When one of them bounced over to me, I stopped crying.

I read the Tao Te Ching: "Simplify your problems. Let go. Let flow."

I scrubbed our floors and cleaned, cleaned, cleaned. I found maggots in the pantry and destroyed them. I tried to go on a bike ride with both Julie and Rena, our dog, but something was wrong with my bike chain, and I didn't know how to fix it.

As Julie, a beautiful blonde little girl, fed herself Cheerios, bits of cheese, and pieces of fruit, I realized that I would rather give up my desire to be 'first' in Jamie's heart than give up the possibility to realize my own loving-ness, my own calm, my own paying-attention, my own grace. These were more important. The only thing that can overcome an addiction (like smoking, or even to another person) is the realization that one is truly freer without it. An even harder lesson is that one can only do this for oneself, and that one might need periodically to resist a "former" addiction again and again.

Julie was standing all the time now. She was compelled to do it by that part of her that sensed the possibility of increased mobility and freedom. For ten times one night, not able to sit down after standing up, she cried for rescue. Ten times I showed her how to get down, and tucked her in. Immediately forgetting her fear, she'd stand again.

The effort of this new freedom was enormous. And she didn't even see the freedom implicit in this step toward walking. Yet she grew toward it instinctively and surely, her effort a silent confirmation that my effort, though I might fall and bang my head, lose my balance or my nerve, was worthwhile and that perseverance would naturally unfold to me the freedom that was already, was always, mine. And so my daughter—and not for the last time—taught *me*, as I picked up The Queen of Cups and started to learn how to make her sing.

The next day the man on eBay raised his price by $50 and the dulcimer, the "Queen of Cups," is now his. He wrote that he had indeed enjoyed my story and hoped that everything had "turned out all right" for me and my daughter. I assured him that it had.

Six:

Framed in Gold

There is a photo I have of Angela: one she used as a publicity shot for her poetry when she was in her early fifties. She is sitting at the small table by a window in her kitchen, set for two, with a big welcoming smile on her face, hands folded in her lap, and a beautiful rope of beads wrapped around her neck. The half of her face away from the window is in shadow. I have framed it in gold. It sits in my bookcase on top of her seven chapbooks of poetry.

I had first met Angela, another poet and teacher of English comp at a nearby UW extension college, sometime in 1973 at a party for (mainly male) English graduate students and famous visiting "deconstructionists" (the literary fad of the day). At that party and, later, when I spent a weekend at her apartment after a bad week with Jamie, I bathed in the solace of female companionship and realized how much I had missed it.

Angela was married to a locally-prominent painter at that time and was extremely concerned that his artistic success not eclipse her own. Her mother had committed suicide by hanging when Angela was 19. Angela was the one who had found her body and had attributed her suicide to the sacrificing of her "voice" and her "art" to traditional marriage and children. Angela had vowed never to let that happen to her, so she worked at her poetry and teaching hard, all the time, and was invested in the hope, in light of the burgeoning women's movement, that all the women she knew did the same. In 1973, the year we met, she published a chapbook called *Who is the Jack?* in which this poem to her mother appeared:

For My Mother, Who Hanged Herself, January 1965

My mother had a devastating laugh.
I heard it peal hah hah hah late at night.
Her raucous amusement made me laugh
to myself in the dark.
I imagined her cigarette burning
as she clutched her knees tight
and opened her inch wide mouth

Eyes closed, neck bent back,
I waited half awake 'til it stopped

The two of us agreed to do a poetry reading together later that winter, and another friend offered me time to read poetry on her radio show. The poetry reading in January of 1974 with Angela and another woman went well, with about 75 paying customers (50 cents each). Several made a point of coming up to me afterward to tell me what especially they liked. This was a new experience for me as I had never before read my own poetry in my own, authentic voice before an audience. I was encouraged enough by that experience (and by Angela) to send some of my poems to publishers. I soon developed a little crush on Angela, who was a few years older than I. Consciously or unconsciously, I saw her as a version of the sister I had lost so long ago. I loved her sense of style, her playfulness, her laugh, and her apparent fearlessness. She was a person who, if she chose, could enjoy herself with almost anyone, anywhere. She was strongly opinionated and sometimes quick to jump to conclusions and generalizations about people, but more often than not, her insights cut deep and true. She was never deliberately cruel and was always willing to revise her opinion if need be. She was ambitious. In essence, she didn't want to be wherever she was now ten years down the line—poetry-wise, I assume. She was blunt and— an odd word springs to mind—resourceful. She had a compulsion about neatness and tidiness that was almost old-maidish or virginal. Yet she saw that in herself and sometimes seemed to parody it.

I learned a lot from just watching her—about directness, drive, spontaneity, 'elegance' and 'professionalism.' Her bluntness annoyed me sometimes, but never for long. Jamie thought her a bit obtuse and unfeeling, and didn't think much of her poetry—but then he too was pretty opinionated.

I learned more about poetry by talking with her rather than just working by myself. At one point we were both reading (and perhaps teaching) Virginia Woolf's diaries. "Observe," Woolf writes, "and use everything." Of my own work, I wrote,

> *Ultimately I have confidence in my teaching and intellectual powers although I'm not sure that's where my ultimate 'work' lies. I have already written more poems this year than all other years together, but still don't feel 'professional' about it. The readings have been good, forcing and enabling me to come out in the open. But a lack of positive feedback hinders. I rarely revise, especially when I sense no particular audience. I'm not*

61

sure it's laziness, just a sense that I'm still exploring what my poetry does, what I want it to do, and how it can be made to do what it does better. I think I've learned some about economy (within sentences), line breaks, and impact (though in no schooled way). I've moved, recently, from the more metaphysical 'power' poems to ones more mundane and ones more immediately and directly involved with our relationship. I tend to start in prose, then snip away, revising three-four drafts at a time, until something halfway resembling a poem emerges. Images are sometimes too obscure, deliberately jarring syntax can be hard to follow, abstract density is sometimes too great (sometimes, alternately, too prosy) and the word disjunctions and word play are often too opaque and/or 'cute.' Reading other poetry more often inspires my own quickly-written poems instead of really helping me technically. I would like, in the abstract, to deal with a greater variety of subjects and people, but it seems that unless I'm feeling something strongly, the poem comes off as weak, 'occasional'. Yet, craft is important—how much or in what way, I'm not sure—and it's difficult consciously to craft in the midst of emotion. I have no 'rules of craft' at this point anyway—only instinct (i.e. this sounds, looks, feels 'right').

This was before the days of MFAs in Creative Writing. What I didn't know, working mainly alone, was that all artists—self-taught or not—learn in the way I was describing. And having a little feedback—from Angela, from my readings—gave me a sense of audience and accountability for the first time. Ultimately, Angela did get an MFA from one of the early programs available. One fall she left for the U. of Massachusetts and was gone for the long periods of required residency, though we kept up a vigorous correspondence by letter. Unfortunately, her marriage to the painter broke up during this time. She reported that her husband had become so jealous of her time alone that she felt unbearably stifled—

needed the freedom to move and grow. She needed to be herself, yet resentment was destroying both of them in the context of their relationship

As Jamie and I started to try to have a child, this became a source of contention between me and Angela, who had given up one child and aborted another because she believed that having children limited a woman's artistic output and could even lead to her death (she still blamed her mother's death on her father's not acknowledging her art and insisting that she have so many children). Yet Angela admitted that, childless, she needed to compensate three/four times over in other areas. She wrote in a letter, "If I choose not to have a child, where am I going to put that energy?" And it didn't go into her marriage, but into her job, her poetry, her endless projects, and her friends/acquaintances.

Shortly before I first gave birth, Angela began to speak of the way it had been with her nearly sixteen years before, when she had had to cut herself off from the reality of her own pregnancy. Not only did she have to hide herself away from her family for nine months, but she had to deny the reality of the birth to *herself*. She said she remembered tiny legs between hers (the child was breech) before she was 'put out.' When she woke up, of course, the child had been taken away, and Angela was given a shot to dry up her milk. She was 19. Decades later, Angela would re-connect with her daughter through a program for reuniting adopted children with their birth mothers, but by that time, her daughter did not want as intimate a relationship as did Angela.

Angela supported herself teaching writing courses at UW-Whitewater and eventually started a magazine: *Sackbut Review*, which she kept running, on her own, for many years. Mainly she used it to promote writers that she believed in, including me. Although I was ultimately getting more pleasure from my poetry than from my academic work, I kept pounding out more pages of my revised dissertation, which I thought would lead to a steady job that would support me and my daughter, if it came to that.

All my relationships changed as a result of my motherhood: I felt suddenly alienated from Angela, sensing in her a mixture of pity and disapproval whenever she came over, though she was always fond of Julie. Her literary magazine continued to do well; she had a relatively well-paying and secure teaching job and was even, one year, listed in *Who's Who in American Women*.

During the times when Angela was in town, there were promises of poetry readings in the fall at a women's prison and even the Performing Arts Center. Some of my poems were published, and Angela, another poet, and I were featured in a new journal called *Lakes and Prairies*. I was asked to write a brief essay about my poetry for the issue. About that time I also submitted my dissertation for final review. There is

another picture of Angela and me: Angela was a sister figure—a sister who saw, loved, cared, and understood, yet asked nothing and was completely different from me. She once said we were like "Braque and Picasso." I loved her similarity and loved her difference: the part that laughed so raucously, that enjoyed people so viscerally, probed so delightfully and irreligiously, that grinned contagiously when suggesting an 'adventure.' I loved the part that could lower her horns like the ram (like my sister, she was a fire sign), ready to do battle if a cause, a feeling, or something/someone she cared for was hurt or attacked. The part that so unselfconsciously created beauty around her—-in design, in space, in time, in the slow cadence of her Southern speech. The slender, shy boy-part of her. The slim body beneath the kimono. The clean floors. The curly hair. The languorous eyes that were pure female. The adolescent whose sometime clumsiness was pure grace. The part that could sniff out opportunity, fun, success, adventure. The part ready to follow up on any interesting or promising trail; the part that was not easily discouraged by dead-ends. The part that enjoyed life so intensely, actively, and profoundly.

I loved the part of her that was woman—who nourished, calmed, understood, helped, held. The part who understood intuitively, even if words on the surface (even hers) got in the way. The part that was first to admit if she'd been wrong. The part that was so clean and straight-forward—to whom deviousness was antithetical. The one who could become lost in a mandala, a plant, a ray of sun, any spot of beauty. She savored it, let it go, yet shared it along the way.

She taught me to take curtains off my windows. To create some measure of beauty around me in my home. To touch in friendship. To be more open to adventure. To have time. I loved her wildness and her calm. She was someone who would always grow more beautiful. I hoped throughout my life always to keep stumbling across her beauty.

*   *   *

I am doing that now, forty years later, twenty years after her suicide by hanging. She killed herself in the summer of 1997, only six weeks after her second "marriage." She was 55 and believed that she had had too high expectations, that she would never become the famous poet she had once envisioned. She said in a letter that she had burned all of her journals, which she earlier had seen as part of her written legacy, but now seeing only "ego and libido" in them. Her mood swings were becoming dangerous, but she resisted any kind of medication, believing that she, like her mother, were victims of the patriarchy, not of the disease of manic depression.

After her divorce in the 70s, she began to take a series of younger lovers, whom she could control. She seemed pleased when I married my third husband, Ben, in 1984, and even when we had a child, Rebecca, late that year. And then, in early 1987, I realized that I was again pregnant. But in February, I caught the stomach flu and had a high fever for several days, after which I miscarried. Ben and I were both very sad, but that loss was one more thing that bonded us.

As it bonded Ben and me, however, it drove me apart from my old friend Angela. Our friendship had survived my marriage to Ben and Rebecca's birth. However, distrusting the demands of husbands and children, believing that they destroyed (or at least interfered greatly with) a woman's own artistic abilities and creativity, Angela was disgruntled when I told her that I was pregnant again. When I told her I had miscarried, she let me know that she thought that was probably a good thing. Of course, she was just stating outright what I was fearing myself. It was therefore perhaps no surprise when I became very angry with her, considering our friendship over, there and then. To her credit, she continued to try to maintain the relationship, both with me and our children.

By the time she was 52, she was not quite so critical of my choices, having felt the need for home and family herself. She took steps to contact the child she gave up for adoption at 19, and showed more inclination for a permanent relationship. Together, we agreed that it was hard to sustain energy and enthusiasm in teaching the same courses, semester after semester.

At one point I had a dream about judging all the people I thought had injured me in one way or another. I was sitting in a judge's chair, but it was much too large for me. In front of my huge judge's desk passed all those with whom I was angry: my mother, Jamie, Angela. The message in the dream was very clear: though I was not "bad" for being angry, I just did not have a large enough perspective to reach a just verdict. That dream helped a lot.

Angela, however, at 54, was not doing well. In November, she called me, talking about "checking out"— suicide. After a long talk she seemed somewhat better, but her depression seemed related to long-unresolved issues over her mother's suicide. In the midst of menopause, Angela realized that she must find/create a new identity independent of herself as 'super achiever.' She was resistant to advice and seemed ensconced in anxiety and despair. I knew there was little I could really do, but when a friendship—even a troubled one— goes back 25 years, it's difficult to remain indifferent. In late December I went to see her. She said she'd been 'shedding her skin'—could see clearly past mistakes she'd made and wanted to change but didn't yet know how. She said she could 'do it herself' and didn't need therapy.

In the spring that she turned 55, Angela and her much younger lover were "married" alongside the Milwaukee River. Though there was indeed a ceremony, Angela never made the marriage legal by signing the necessary forms. Another sign of her distrust of marriage was in her choice of men: he deferred to her in everything. Far from having an equal relationship, Angela refused to let go of the reins at all. More and more uncomfortable with her plummeting mood, to my discredit, I avoided Angela in the six weeks after her wedding and before her suicide.

Ultimately, Angela succumbed to the battle with mental illness, and, for many years after her death on July 23, 1997, instead of seeing her through the lens of "feminine compassion," I judged her, like Marilyn, for leaving me. Unable, as she once said, to "get the dress of old age over her head," unhappy in the not-quite-real marriage she had undertaken in late May, faced with the many debts thereof, and believing her artistic life to have been a failure— instead of the "dress" of old age, she slipped a noose around her head in the basement of the home she had bought and paid for by herself. She was 55, the same age at which her mother had also hung herself, according to Angela, because her creative talents had been destroyed by her roles of wife and mother.

My anger at her death no doubt masked, for a time, my grief for her and my fears about my own choices in life. I did help organize the memorial right after her death, in which I expressed, in part, my anger. Did she have to choose the perception that led her to believe she had to redeem her mother's death by being a 'super achiever?' (At that point I was still only vaguely aware that I had *also* been trying to "redeem" the stunted lives of my sister and my mother.) I did not want to see Angela as a victim with no choices, yet neither did I want to sit in judgment of her, though I did. I wanted to believe that, even if she was bi-polar (whatever that meant), in the end she could have chosen differently. Was that asking too much?

Still I knew that she had persevered in our friendship, even when I did not, and that she had pulled me, even at her funeral, into the Milwaukee community of poets who also mourned her death and sought to find meaning in it.

August brought more responsibility at work in addition to finishing the summer session. I had little time to process Angela's death, even as I was facing issues similar to hers.

Marriage, in my experience, was difficult, especially for a woman. Like Angela, I felt the patriarchal limitations on me as an aging woman. I felt no longer even passably attractive, and that really hurt because a young, beautiful, fertile woman has everything our culture admires, particularly if she's 'successful' and ambitious as well (new 'musts'). Neither Angela nor I achieved the worldly 'success' we had once hoped for, though unlike me, she never stopped trying until she hanged herself when her best efforts clearly weren't enough.

I keep thinking of her phrase: she just couldn't get that "dress of old age" over her head. The "new" role of Crone: the wise woman, spiritual teacher, healer to which we give lip service gets 'stuck' over most of our heads: such wisdom must still come in a beautiful package. In 1997 I saw myself as wrinkled and fat by the beauty standards of the day. I was starting to look like my own mother, whose physical features (plump body, gray hair) I had always disdained. I had chosen the "feminist" path of not using hormones, hair dye, or dieting to make me look younger. And then I felt undesirable. I didn't tear up my journals, but I did tear up most photographs of myself and wanted no one to take my picture. Even then I admitted that all this was vanity

—in both senses of the word: narcissistic and useless—and yet I seemed to be making little headway against it. And I despised myself for that. But I did not kill myself, I thought, a little too smugly.

And then I thought that this was perhaps my challenge: simply not to give up—on myself, on other people. And yet a part of me (an 'old' part) simply despaired, wanting to quit, disbelieving in the kind of intimacy and nurturance I'd once experienced with my sister as a child.

When my mother died after a heart bypass operation in 1980, Angela wrote me a poem, which she later included in her *Book of Charms* (Barnwood Press, 1983), which, along with eight other beautiful books—*Who is the Jack?* (1973), *Letters from Lee's Army* (Morgan Press, 1979), *Discovering the Mandala* (Lakes and Prairies Press, 1981), *Refreshing the Fey* (Sackbut Press, 1986), *A Heathen Herbal* (Peaceable Press, 1986), *Remembering Rivers* (Sackbut Press, 1991), *Always Improving My Appetite* (Sackbut Press, 1994), and *Singing a Circle of Seasons* (Sackbut Press, 1995)—will always remain on my shelf with her photograph, smiling in her kitchen, half of her face in shadow.

Grief Charm for Kathleen

Here there is unseasonal snow,
white covering the new green grass,
an achy Monday
when no one wants to go out.
As I walk your dog
the seventh day,
tonight on icy streets

69

I think what perfect weather
for organ music.

You must have heard some
in the little Kansas town
you brought her back to,
after nights spent
on hospital sofas
amid the hum of strangers' comments,
the last of restaurant soup

with the 2 crackers in cellophane,
motel towels, colored television.

She closed veins, mouth, eyes,
her history. You closed
the issues of sugared treats,
Bible stories, or whether
you should force a child to eat.
You felt an end to being daughter enough
for a woman who once had two.

You, in the old house,
were taller, the furniture
smaller, and her things
took on a strange aura
as if on exhibit in a museum.

Though you will have to weep
for when you didn't listen
and didn't want to kiss,
and will suddenly find
much about her precious
and mysterious, I want you to
even more value yourself,

her pain pulling
the words of balm you do possess,
your energy to clean, fold, feed,
encourage and make arrangements.
Words to remind father and child
the cycle of growth this represents.
And the words for yourself
that will not only help but enhance.

And you will begin again
as you have had to do before
and you will know that change
is the sprouting bulb
in the border of loss.

Ghost
(for Angela)

On the far side of the theater in the round
surrounded by summer oaks, cicadas, whippoorwills,
warm breeze drowsy, billowing the cloth of the set,
she sits alone in the first row, shoes off,
loafing and enjoying herself, laughing at
the fool's jokes though the play is a tragedy,
slim, slouching in the comfortable heat then leaning
forward, rapt, chin in hands, elbows on knees
spread wide across the sleeveless light-blue dress
and my throat tightens, knowing it isn't you,
can't possibly be you, but,
not able to make out her features, how
like you used to be she is, and,
abruptly conjured from the trap door of my heart,
from underneath the worn edge of my outrage
at your self-murder twelve years gone,
without warning rises the sharpness of how much,
how much I miss your outrageous laugh,
our youth, the lanky ease of your fierce company.

Seven:

The Escape Hatch

In 1979, during the time in which I was a single mother, I was drawn more and more to a group of women, many of them poets and artists, who were starting a "coven." We first gathered on February 2, Candlemas, the festival of Brigid, goddess of poetry (among other things). There were eight of us, led by Sue. Many of them were lapsed Catholics and feared ritual; as a lapsed Methodist, I craved it. Simply, we lit a candle and passed it around in a short ritual of wishing. I wished for light and celebration at a time when I too often became angry and impatient with the world, my daughter, and with myself. I wished for the power to transform. We would meet again at the new moon. Several members mentioned the importance of such groups in a time of world crisis—when Cambodians were starving and the media was speaking casually of WWII as if it had never happened. There was indeed a need of light; however, no one else in any other aspect of my life knew about my involvement in this group.

We did not even call ourselves "witches," though we were practicing Wicca.

On my 35th birthday, I had another rotten cold—the third in six weeks. Julie had been sick too, and we were snarling at each other for three days. I was given notice by Marquette that I would not be re-hired in the fall, mainly because of my many absences, due to my mother's death in April, 1980, and my daughter's many childhood sicknesses. I believed that this was unfair, but was also relieved that I would not have to teach there again. Doing some calculations I realized that, with unemployment compensation and what I'd saved, we would be OK for about 18 months. After my mother's death, my father and I drew a little closer, visiting each other several times a year. At 70 he had definitely mellowed, was a good grandfather to Julie, and gave us luxuries like a small washer and dryer that I couldn't afford on my own.

I did some further self-talk. I told myself that I possessed qualities other than sheer brutish survival: qualities like vibrancy, a capacity for joy, and passion. I sought renewal with the coming spring equinox, and while I knew that what I sought could only be found within me, it often seemed like such a gargantuan task to even look.

The coven met again at full moon, and we each shared a story. I spoke of my experiences at Bird Mound. I fell a little in love with Sue—another sister figure—with the openness and purity of the channel that she was. The coven met both of my then-current needs: to be seen by like-minded others, and to remain hidden from those who were not like-minded.

Parenting continued to be a challenge. Julia's being 2 ½ was no fun. Though she was becoming easier to converse with, was often quite funny and loving, she had spells of temper and unreasonableness that were quite difficult to bear. If I wasn't too tired, I could see past them, but if I was sick or fatigued (which I often was), I blew up too and there was a real conflagration.

Since I had no one else to consult (most of the "Wiccans" were childless or had much older children), I turned to books like *Whole Child, Whole Parent* (Polly Berrien Berends, 1975), to the *I Ching* , and to Tarot and astrology. All of them were teachers. I typed up and put on my mirror a passage from *WCWP* that I still have taped to my mirror, decades later, and which I still need occasionally to read:

> *Love is the sorting out in thought of the perfect child from all suggestions to the contrary. The child who is held in thought to his [sic] errors will manifest them steadfastly. He[sic] cannot do otherwise. But a clear picture of the perfect child in the parent's consciousness, which sees (un-sees) all imperfections as irrelevant to the child's true being allows the child to develop truthfully with the speediest and most effortless falling away of all irrelevant behavior.*
>
> *Just as we can see purity right in the middle of the diaper mess, so also must we learn to see gentleness in the middle of the violence, innocence in the face of guile, perfection where imperfection seems to be, intelligence where there appears to be stupidity, goodness and the desire to be good right where there seems to be willful badness.*
>
> *These qualities of purity, innocence, intelligence, gentleness, and goodness are true. Whenever we see them, we see God (good). When we find them in our children, we discover them in ourselves. When we see them clearly and discover them everywhere, we begin to see that they are true—not as personal virtues but as the truth of being. When we see that they are true, we are conscious.*

Even today I cannot re-read those words without tears springing to my eyes. It is a message I need to repeat over and over again.

They contrast greatly with a journal called "My Escape Hatch" (1967-1970) written by my mother, Clara, and hidden away under her dresser drawer lining to be found by me in

1980 after her death. It gave me new insight as well as a new kind of sadness concerning the many losses and disappointments of her life, including me. Here are some excerpts:

Jan. 6,'67: As always after Kathleen has been home for a while and left to go back to school, the house seems so awfully quiet and so empty! I wonder about their New Year party .. .! do hope there was no liquor. How I wish I could protect her from all the evil in this world .... I'm lonely and feel my life is so barren. How I wish we could have had more children! Surely things would have been different had Marilyn lived. Of course, if she had, now at 31 she would be in a home of her own, but there would be visits and grandchildren .... Have been trying to think of something I could do that Leonard would approve and wouldn't cost too much. I have considered taking organ lessons. I do love music and do wish I could really play. I am so happy the Lord gave Kathleen musical talent and the fine mind she has and do hope that someday she will use them for His Glory.

1/13/67: I know she is so very busy and doesn't have much time to write, but her letters and phone calls mean so much to me. When we don't hear anything for a long time, I think too much and with no one to talk to, I'm afraid I get to thinking in a twisted sort of way. Have given up taking any classes at the YWCA. The ones I was really interested in meet at night and certainly don't want to go alone. Besides there is a $5 fee to join the Y which is compulsory besides a fee for each class. And it would be no fun to go alone. How I wish I had even one real friend! Have never been able to make and keep friends. There is surely something about me that people don't like. If I only knew what it was, would certainly quit whatever it is. But I honestly don't know why I don't have any friends. Even one would make a real difference.

1/18/67: I'm sorry I got to feeling so resentful about Leonard working in the basement. He has been working on something for the telephone co. which will be a feather in his cap besides his thoroughly enjoying doing it. Guess I'm just basically selfish. Evidently the plan to get together for bridge with .... fell through. Far be it from me to push three unwilling people into doing something they don't want to do!. .. suppose will have to build as satisfying life as I can, solitary as it will be.

2/1/67: [after not helping her niece who was a battered woman] 1 have failed everyone I have ever loved in some way. I don't know why. Guess I'm not a strong enough character or good enough Christian. At times I have terrible guilt feelings. I failed and hurt Mama. That is just a start. It's been everyone I love, at one time or another. No wonder I have no friends. If I was someone else, I wouldn't like me either!! ... 1t grieves me that Kathleen and I are not close. God knows I want to be and have always wanted to. I don't have the understanding or tact that it takes. There are times Kathleen completely baffles me but still I love her dearly. But it has always been and always will be a great hurt to me that we are not close. Suppose it is mostly my fault, but there it is again. What is it???

2/9/67: When I was working [after my sister's death, as a part-time bookkeeper], I felt that I was contributing financially so we could give Kathleen a good education. But now, when I have more time to think, I wonder if I was doing the right thing? Certainly if I had not worked, IF we had any savings at all for retirement, we couldn't have sent Kathleen to Ohio Wesleyan. It is an expensive school. But now I'm not at all sure I was right. If we had had less available money, Kathleen would have either had to have gone here, or at least closer to home. I feel that she has grown so far away from us since she has gone to college .... did she have to change so completely to where she can't be happy with us anymore? I wonder if I hadn't worked, if Kathleen and I would be closer. Maybe, but

I can't really believe it, I just don't know. Even from the time she could talk she exerted her own personality definitely!! There was so much difference between her and Marilyn. Oh how I wish Marilyn could have lived. I wish Kathleen could have known her. Even though Kathleen was 7 years old, she says she doesn't even remember her. Marilyn loved her little sister so much.

3/6/67 [wishing she had a bigger house]: *Of course, I could suggest we sell the organ and would have more room but can't bring myself to do that. I know I can't play well and never will, but I do really enjoy it when I'm here alone. Don't really have nerve enough to play for anyone but Leonard. As I know I can't play very well and besides no one has ever asked me to. I'm sorry Kathleen has never liked it. We could have had such fun playing piano and organ duets. She has always acted like it pained her to play with me when I asked her. Can't help but think at times how much Marilyn would have enjoyed it. It hurts that we weren't able to give Marilyn much, we never even got the new piano until after she was sick.*

3/15/67: *Kathleen is 22 today! It doesn't really seem so long since she was a tiny baby, and Marilyn so happy over the baby sister she had wanted so very much ... and how early Kathleen's independence asserted itself!! her "NO!! DO MYSELF!!!" Well, I guess she is still that way. but how often I felt like paddling her! I love her dearly .... 1 know or feel that I haven't been a good mother, and it grieves me. Wish I knew how to be. Guess the Good Lord knew what He was doing when He just gave me two children and took one back so soon instead of the large family I always felt that I wanted. It would have just been that many more to have failed ....*

3/30/67: *I do miss Kathleen, she had so much reading to do and with Luke here too, don't feel that I really had a visit with her at all. . .I doubt if she will be home this summer. I know she won't if she can help it. She has applied for a job with*

"Upward Bound." Suppose I imagine things probably because I'm alone so much and think too much but it looks to me that she doesn't want to be home with us anymore ....

4/24/67: Just what does a person DO when all the work is done, and you have nowhere to go or no one to even talk to?? If it was the one day like that, there would be no problem, but I have hours and hours every day like that.

5/4/67: [on not being able to afford to come to my Phi Beta Kappa initiation]: Sometimes I wonder. why did she want so very much to go to school so far away from home? Could it possibly be that she is ashamed of us and doesn't want us to keep coming to her school? Would we embarrass her by being there? Leonard offered to let me go back on an airplane ... I said no because I was afraid. He just floors me!! After preaching how hard up we are and we must quit unnecessary spending, and I have been careful—haven't had my hair fixed, no new clothes. Then offers to spend $150 just like that!! Sometimes I can't figure him out.

6/19/67: [after I screamed at my father for hitting with a newspaper the dog I had given him]: It seems so odd and so wrong that loving her as much as we do that there is such a great gulf or wall between us. It's very doubtful now if things will ever be any different. At times she acts like I get on her nerves and am disgusting to her. I don't know how else to act, I'm just me. Maybe I am a person who is repulsive to others. That's probably why I have no friends .... Leonard and Kathleen were mad, and I was so hurt over it all I was miserable, even all day yesterday. The sermon at church was "guilt and forgiveness." Kathleen wouldn't go. It seems I carry such a load of guilt. I KNOW I am not a good mother and never have been. I am too weak and hate violence in any form. I would rather give in than to have a scene. I never have disciplined either Marilyn or Kathleen as I should have on occasions. Marilyn's temperament was so different from

79

Kathleen. She was a great deal like me. But with K. I think it couldn't... .. There must be something the matter with me that I can't settle myself down. I just hope this restlessness and depression isn't an indication of mental illness... She has always had everything her own way here at home until she apparently has no respect whatsoever for either of us and probably underneath loathes me for my weakness. That is very likely the whole trouble that has caused the rift between us— and it's MY FAULT!!!

7/17/67: Haven't made any progress yet on becoming closer to Kathleen. Suppose it's years too late for that. However it's far more pleasant than last summer was. We play two-handed bridge and gin rummy .... I wish Kathleen wasn't so lonely. How I wish we could come to a close understanding of each other, but then there is the 'generation gap' besides the fact that we have never been close as Marilyn and I were. How it grieves me!

9/6/67: Don't know what to do about volunteering at the hospital. Finally talked to Leonard about it, but all he said was "why in the world would you want to do THAT?" I really had a few doubts in my mind anyway whether or not I really could do it well.

9/15/67: Have about talked myself into thinking I am too old to volunteer in hospital, if only my hair weren't so white. I am afraid of rejection and failure .. When it comes time to do it, something holds me back and in the end, I do nothing. I've always felt inferior to other people .... Suppose the winter will be a repeat of television, reading, housework, and boredom!! Some days I don't mind it so much and other days can hardly stand it.

9/25/67: Today it has been 15 years and one month since Marilyn left us. It's been like an eternity. I still miss her and I love her so much. I hope she knows.

1/3/68: *Have been thinking back over this last year and my life. I don't like particularly what I see in myself and surely most of my lifetime is spent and for what? I have done nothing for anyone. Nor anything of which I can be proud. I might just as well not have been born, for anything that I have accomplished. And to be perfectly honest, I know I have inflicted hurt on most people who I have loved the most....after 57 years of selfish living can it be done?*

1/24/68: *I looked for Kathleen to call Monday night. She had begged off from calling when she got home Sun as it would be late and she would be tired, so really looked for her to call Monday, but she did not call. When Leonard found out I felt so bad and was worried about her he put through a call at 10:30—11:30 there. She had been asleep and didn't know she was supposed to call!!*

2/8/68: *I haven't accomplished anything ... I kidded myself when I was teaching Sunday school and had K's GS troop that I was doing something useful. Had hoped some of the girls would like me enough to keep in touch, but none of them have. My papa used to say that God had a plan for everyone's life. If that is true, how I wish I knew what He intended for me to do ... lf I had had the same opportunity for schooling that Kathleen has had I would have liked to have entered nurse's training after high school but with Mama and me at home I needed to earn money anyway I could. Instead of spending it on education, paying the rent and buying groceries and coal was more important! Oh well. ... I wouldn't have been a good nurse anyway. I would probably have flubbed that like I have everything else. I have always felt that a woman could be fulfilled and find her meaning in life through making a home for her husband and children and I still think so if the woman is a good wife and a good mother. But when there is nothing but failure and shallowness underneath the front the world sees there is just nothing there ....*

81

5/9/68: I can tell she isn't really happy with us here ... she never has been. Oh how I wish we could have had more children!!! and that Kathleen and I could have had a close relationship, but it seems she has always held me off at arm's length and never let me be close to her.

7/1/68 {after my marriage}: I feel that I have embarked on another phase of my life and it's surely either the next to the last one or the last one. My life is nearly over. The first was when I was a child at home. We were poor, but I didn't realize it. I can truthfully say I had a happy childhood even though we didn't have much money. I began to realize that more as I got into high school. I was never popular but I did have a few friends and dated, even though I didn't have very many clothes. It was worse after Papa died in my senior year in high school. The second phase was shorter, while I was working after graduation. Mama and I were living at home alone. The depression was upon us, and if it hadn't been for [her brother] helping us, we could never have lived on my $11 or $12 a week I made. Leonard and I wanted to get married but Mama was sick and didn't want me to. I'll never cease being sorry that I didn't wait, but oh no I wanted to get married! It broke up her home and she was so sick, I didn't realize at the time, how sick she was or don't think I would have done it. She lived less than a year and that is one of the things I feel so guilty about.
The third phase was our early married years before Marilyn was born. I was happy, even though it was at my sick mother's expense. The depression was still with us and there was no doubt about it, I knew we were poor then!. ...
The next phase was motherhood. I wanted a baby so very, very much. We really couldn't afford one. I lost one before I got pregnant with M. I loved her very very much and I still do, to this day, nearly 16 years after her death!.. ..... 1 wanted another baby. I lost another one. Then I got pregnant again with K. I was ecstatic .... Then we moved to Wichita, and Marilyn was heartbroken, leaving all her friends. She was

such a friendly, warm outgoing, lovable girl she had a lot of friends. How I wish Kathleen could have known her. ...
The next phase I believe came when we lost M to polio ..... My world was coming down on top of me. Utterly crushed in my sorrow, don't think I was a very good mother to Kathleen. The day we took Marilyn to the hospital, I completely forgot Kathleen! God was surely looking after her. She was only 7 and was in the car alone in the parking lot for at least 5 hours before I suddenly remembered her. She hadn't had any lunch. I didn't want to do anything but nurse my grief and cry ..... [talks about going to work as a bookkeeper]. I could buy cute dresses for Kathleen while at the same time my heart ached because I couldn't buy pretty clothes for Marilyn .... I believe if I hadn't worked we would never have had the money to have sent her to OWU and she would have gone here or at least in Kansas and maybe lived closer.

This journal was (and still is) incredibly painful for me to read—not only about her assessment of me, but of herself. There were sections where she did seem to understand some of what I was going through and wished that she could help, but of course I focused on the ones that confirmed the pain I myself had felt about our relationship. I believed that her life had been stunted by many things, including patriarchal attitudes like those of my father and by clinical depression. Given the times, there was no way to "undo" all that. She was right—there was too much of a "generation gap" between us. As I write this, at age 71, I am 14 years older than she was when she wrote it. I feel only sadness and a great compassion for her. There were many times when she off-handedly revealed to me that she wanted something, like a new set of dishes. But she would not ask my father for them because she said he would make light of her request and refuse it. More than once, I took this information straight to my father and demanded that he give her what she wanted. He seemed surprised, but acquiesced.

Thirty years after my mother wrote her "escape hatch," in which she expressed her painful feelings of helplessness, I read that people with severe anxiety/depression often draw pictures of themselves without hands. It reminded me, not only of my mother, but of the recent dream I'd shared with my psychiatrist about a "severed hand" taking root in my garden as well as the fairy tale called "The Handless Maiden." Here is part of Wikipedia's summary of that tale:

A miller was offered wealth by the devil if the miller gave him what stood behind the mill. Thinking that it was an apple tree, the miller agreed, but it was his daughter. When three years had passed, the devil appeared, but the girl had kept herself sinless and her hands clean, and the devil was unable to take her. The devil threatened to take the father if he did not chop off the girl's hands, and she let him do so, but she wept on her arms' stumps, and they were so clean that the devil could not take her, so he had to give her up. She set out into the world, despite her father's wealth. She saw a royal garden and wanted to eat some pears she saw there. An angel helped her. The pears were missed the next day, and the gardener told how she appeared. The king awaited her the next day and when she came again, married her and made her hands out of silver.

The meaning of this fairy tale can be debated, but I am drawn to Anne Sexton's female-centered version in her book *Transformations (1971)*. Here is the first part of the poem:

THE MAIDEN WITHOUT HANDS

*Is it possible
he marries a cripple
out of admiration?
A desire to own the maiming
so that not one of us butchers*

84

will come to him with crowbars
or slim precise tweezers?
Lady, bring me your wooden leg
so I may stand on my own
two pink pig feet.
If someone burns out your eye
I will take your socket
and use it for an ashtray.
If they have cut out your uterus
I will give you a laurel wreath
to put in its place.
If you have cut off your ear
I will give you a crow
who will hear just as well.
My apple has no worm in it!
My apple is whole!
Once
there was a cruel father
who cut off his daughter's hands
to escape from the wizard.
The maiden held up her stumps
as helpless as dog's paws
and that made the wizard
want her. He wanted to lap
her up like strawberry preserve.
She cried on her stumps
as sweet as lotus water,
as strong as petroleum,
as sure-fire as castor oil.
Her tears lay around her like a moat.
Her tears so purified her
that the wizard could not approach.
She left her father's house
to wander in forbidden woods,
the good, kind king's woods.
She stretched her neck like an elastic,
up,, up,, to take a bite of a pear

hanging from the king's tree.
Picture her there for a moment,
a perfect still life.
After all,
she could not feed herself
or pull her pants down
or brush her teeth.
She was, I'd say,
without resources. [. . .]

"Without resources" is how I would describe my mother's view of herself as well as my view of myself at certain times in my life. I also have come to believe that there is a gender effect in how one's helplessness is learned/perceived/encouraged.

Nevertheless, my mother, with the hands she had, made great fried chicken and peach pie, and she took great pains to teach me how. She coaxed beautiful petunias, zinnias, and roses out of the harsh Kansas clay. She knew the names of countless birds and constellations.

Her house was spotless.

Picking Peaches

My mother remembered one beautiful day.
She made pilgrimage with others to pick bushels
of peaches in the public orchard, and after,
she would can jam and bake pies,

but that wasn't the point. The point was
the glory of that day, the rare harmony
with her husband and their friends, the warmth and
lusciousness of the just-picked fruit.

For once, she allowed herself happiness,
or rather, delight overtook her.
But next year when they returned, angels
of Eden barred the way with swords: the day

wasn't quite as warm, her husband in a
foul mood, the peaches sour, pithy,
overripe. She always talked about
her disappointment as if she just couldn't

understand why, once allowed,
a particular pleasure couldn't be recaptured,
but bounded away into the past.
Yet she rounded up sorrows easily,

pecks of sad skinny cats always
at the back door, a yowling litany
she thought would leave her alone, if she fed them.
Instead, they grew sleek and fat. I saw

they would never leave a good thing
once they found it. My mother-in-law never
used any beautiful thing she was given
but closed them all carefully away in drawers.

Released into dementia, she was never
disappointed by lining up present and past.
"What a beautiful garden," she would exclaim from
our porch, while she could still speak.

a moment later, "What a beautiful garden,"
not knowing she was repeating herself.
The Buddhists say to meditate on death,
so to self-medicate against

forgetfulness of impermanence, a kind
of caffeine or nitroglycerin for the
soul. But like most mothers I have
no need to meditate on impermanence—

have seen moments snatched, fade, sucked
away right before my eyes, have
no belief that today's delights will last
past this turn of the kaleidoscope.

It seems joy is just something we pick.
I used to lick the warm fuzz of dust
off my mother's closed bedroom door.
My mouth still waters at the thought.

Eight:

Twenty-seven Years of Grade Books

Deep inside a box in my closet are twenty-seven years of grade books. I tell myself that I'm keeping them in case, as rarely happens, a student contacts me for a reference. I have written so many letters of recommendation for students, and I have needed those grade books to remind me of not only who they were, but also what kind of student they were. Without them, all of that information would be lost, and my former student would be out of luck.

However, it's been over ten years since I retired, and the last request for a letter came several years ago, so I really have no reason to hold on to them, or all the personal notes from students, or my own evaluations. Or the commemorative clock (which has long since stopped working) on which is engraved my name and the words, "Thank You For 30 Years Of Service To AOC Students And Staff At UWM." I hadn't noticed until just now when I typed it that every last preposition was Incorrectly Capitalized.

After I received my doctorate in 1976, I was kept on, *pro forma*, as a lecturer for two years, but was then cut loose to find my own job at some other school. Unfortunately, I had found only a year stint at Marquette University from '79-'80 as an adjunct lecturer, teaching four sections of tightly prescribed freshman English courses based solely on Aristotelian rhetoric. When I was absent too much due to my own and Julie's sickness and my mother's death, I was perfunctorily fired.

So, living on unemployment for a year, I turned back to writing poetry, spending more time with Julie, and trying to figure out, at age 35, what I would do with the rest of my life. After focusing on what I truly wanted—a job in which I had some freedom to teach in a meaningful way, and a new relationship of equality—both essentially fell into my lap. They seem like two separate stories, but they were and still are intertwined.

In the summer of '81, a male friend and fellow poet knew that I needed a job, and when one opened up in UWM's summer Pre-College Program, he recommended me (he worked for a similar program at the university). It came at a good time, for my funds were running low and my unemployment was running out. The job consisted of teaching an eight-week course to Milwaukee high school students brought to the UWM campus for the program in hopes of recruiting them to UWM after high school graduation. They were largely minority students, with whom I hadn't had much experience, and they were high school students, an age group with which I had unfortunate memories from over a decade ago. Nevertheless, it felt good to have paid work again, and Julie and I still had free summer afternoons when we could go to the beach.

One day in the middle of a class, I got a note asking me to contact the head of the Department of Educational Opportunity. They were looking for an English instructor for the fall, and the same friend (who was an advisor in that department) had again recommended me for the job. I applied, was quickly interviewed, and was hired on the spot. By comparison to today's lengthy application process for even the most minor academic post, it was ridiculously easy. I still had aspirations to something "greater," however, and saw the job as strictly temporary—a fill-in—until something better came along. After all, I was 36 and still hoped to do more with my life than teach uninspiring freshman composition courses forever.

Nevertheless, the working conditions at UWM were so much better than at Marquette. I had a nice office (not just a corner of someone else's), a class assistant to help with paper grading so that I almost never had to bring work home, helpful associates, and intriguing students, much more diverse than any I had ever taught before: not just Caucasian and African-American, but Hispanic, Native-American, and Hmong. Many of them were also older than the traditional 18-year-old college freshman.

The Department of Educational Opportunity at UWM was one of many such centers authorized by the Higher Education Amendments of 1972. An outgrowth of other such programs such as Upward Bound, Talent Search, and Student Support Services—all of which emerged out of the Economic Opportunity Act of 1964 in response to the federal government's War on Poverty—Educational Opportunity programs offered "disadvantaged" (the term was soon deemed pejorative and changed to "underprepared") students intense advising and special sections of math, English, reading, and study skills during their first two years of college, after which, if successful (a big "if" as it turned out), they were "mainstreamed."

At the time I was hired, DEO had been around UWM for about nine years and had an enviable budget with many staff who were as ethnically and racially diverse as the students we served. As a white female with no experience teaching students of color, it is perhaps surprising that I was hired, but not so surprising that I needed a lot of formal and informal education about the learning styles—so different from my own—of the students I taught. However, I found these students, for the most part, very serious about their educations, especially as many of them, like me, were first-generation college students and had much-needed jobs to help support their studies and often their families. Affirmative action was in full swing. Our department had its own admission process, and we often admitted students with ACT scores as low as 12-14, as long as they had other things to recommend them, sometimes no more than a glowing letter from one of their high school teachers. As a staff, we became quite committed to retaining our students, and had many, many staff sessions about "best practices" in order to do so. Unfortunately, despite our university's "urban mission," our department and staff were "ghetto-ized" by the rest of the university. We were all lecturers—second-class faculty with none of the benefits and certainly not the paycheck of the regular "faculty"—and there was an ongoing undercurrent of disdain among many "regular" faculty about whether or not "these students" should be in college at all.

Today, such programs are increasingly rare. The one at UWM closed its doors in 2016. Even though the Supreme Court upheld affirmative action in the same year, changes still obviously need to be made in the ways "financially disadvantaged" and non-Caucasian students are educated in this country.

But such political commitment, advocating, and radicalization were in my future. These were not the reasons I took the job in 1981. I was beginning to feel, at long last, like a respectable, responsible, grown-up. I was thrilled to have a regular paycheck and a three-year contract. Julie was eligible for a free, half-day K-4 program at a Montessori school and was eligible for the university day-care center in the afternoons. We settled into a good routine. I began to regain some confidence in my abilities as a teacher. My evaluations were good, and students seemed to like and appreciate what I had to offer them outside of the "inner worlds and visions" classes I had taught as a graduate student, modeled largely upon what my second husband, Jamie, had been teaching.

* * *

In the fall of '82, I started to think a lot about the advantages and disadvantages of becoming involved again with a man. Part of me still longed for a "real" marriage, and I had been completely celibate for five years. Julie and I were very close, yet I would look enviously upon the couples I saw with their shared, respectable, middle-class lives which I no doubt idealized.

About the same time Julie and I had started to attend regular seasonal festivities and rituals at Circle Sanctuary in the Wisconsin beautiful Driftless (unglaciated) area about 150 miles from Milwaukee. The founder and High Priestess, Selena Fox, became a friend and quickly overcame my lingering doubts about anyone considered to be a "witch." Also helpful were soon-to-become-famous books such as Starhawk's *The Spiral Dance: A Rebirth of the Ancient Religion of the Great Goddess* (1979), Margot Adler's *Drawing Down the Moon: Witches, Druids, Goddess-Worshippers, and Other Pagans in America Today* (1979), *The Politics of Women's Spirituality* (ed. Charlene Spretnak, 1982), and *Mother Wit: A Feminist Guide to Psychic Development* (Marie Mariechild, 1981). Wicca, with its emphasis on feminism, nature, and the Great Mother, seemed a good fit for me.

Since Selena, a certified clinical psychotherapist, was starting a counseling practice in connection to her other magical work, I became her first "telephone" client. For several months, we talked about both my fear and desire for another possible relationship, using imagery and dreams as well as her own considerable psychic powers. I visualized and articulated the kind of relationship I wanted: one of equality and "fidelity." Men were starting to notice me again, but I had not yet encouraged any.

In January of 1983, DEO decided to add a second "pre-requisite" level, English 90, for those students whose background and ability in composition were even lower than those in English 95, already a non-credit course meant to prepare students for the first semester of "regular" English 101. I was called out during a very snowy vacation to attend a meeting on the curriculum for this new course. I was rather surly about it because, not only did I hate meetings in general (still do), but had to find a baby-sitter on short notice for this one.

When I walked into the meeting, late, I noticed that there was only one man there that I had never met before. He did a double-take when he looked at me, which I found amusing and rather intriguing. Turns out, this man had been recently hired to develop the new English 90 curriculum. I remember looking at him scornfully. Just another white male: what could he possibly know about teaching under-prepared students that I didn't already know?

Well, that meeting finally ended, and I thought no more about it. One day, however, after I had been running at the gym and wrestling with the same ambivalent feelings (was I ready for a new relationship or not?), I came to an inner decision. In my mind, I said to the Powers That Be, "All right. I'm ready. If there's someone out there who is right for me, bring him on." I walked back to my office, and there was that English 090 man, Ben, waiting to talk to me, ostensibly about teaching the new class, but as we talked, it became clear that something more was going on.

I was afraid that I knew what it was. He was intensely attractive and seemed just as interested in me. My feelings were so strong that they frightened me. I wanted to back off. When he asked me out for dinner, I said no—despite his curly hair, great body in terrific shape, and blue eyes that were so intense they were almost black. He leaned back easily in the "guest" chair in my office, silently taking my measure as I chattered on about my job and my dreams.

That spring, we ran into each other constantly. We went for walks around campus. My decision not to become involved with him seemed right when I learned that he was on the rebound from a relationship and that he was on his way out of town: he had just been admitted to the prestigious Iowa Writers' Workshop. He was a filmmaker and a fiction writer (apparently in addition to being an English curriculum developer). I was later to discover that he had a history of applying to do just about anything, believing that he could do it just as well and probably better than anyone else (and he was usually right). He seemed intrigued, but not put off when I described myself as a Witch (test one). He seemed interested (but not unnaturally so) when I told him that I had a four-year-old daughter (test two).

In the next few months, I watched myself lose ten pounds and buy myself a new pair of tight jeans and a new diaphragm (what was going on here? he was leaving town!). I agreed to do a poetry reading with a few others and invited Ben. I wrote a poem about my new-found desire, using an apple as an image, and left a copy of the poem and an apple in his university mailbox (what WAS going on here? he was leaving town!).

At the poetry reading, he came in late but in time for that poem. We sat together afterwards and had a glass of wine and couldn't take our eyes off of each other. When I left, he kissed me goodbye. We made a date for the next day when we went to lunch. Since we took my car, I asked him if he could drive a clutch, at which point he just laughed.

He made *me* laugh. My family had been so very serious, and Jamie and I had been so serious, talking exhaustively and analytically about ourselves and our psyches, that not doing so was a relief. A Vietnam-era veteran who had, despite being drafted, surprisingly not been sent to Vietnam, Ben had a distrust of "intellectuals" and the academy, though of course that was one of his professions, and he went on to develop a stellar career as an academic administrator. But at that time, I loved most that he could make me laugh at myself without rancor or embarrassment.

One kink in all of this was that (yes! listen!) he was leaving town. I tried to back-pedal my feelings. It didn't really matter if he left town; things had not yet progressed so far that I would miss him very much if he did leave. By April, that was no longer true. I was falling in love.

Another kink was that I was pretty far along in the process of buying a house. I had always wanted to be a homeowner, so, with some savings (Julie was no longer in day-care), I decided to buy a small house just a few blocks away from the flat where we lived. Even though I was 38 with a steady job, I was a single woman who did not have quite enough money for the down payment, so my father (a man) had to co-sign the mortgage loan. At that time I was just happy that my father agreed to do it (generously signing over his share to me with a "quit claim" and one penny). The negotiations for this house had already taken place by the time I realized how serious my relationship with Ben was becoming, so, on the surface, our future didn't seem at all well-timed.

Yet Ben "fit the bill" for everything I had envisioned. Though he was 18 months younger than I, we seemed to be "equal" in everything that mattered. He had respect for my individuality, believed in being faithful, and was steady in all of the ways that mattered. I noticed such things as his gentleness and attention to Rena and also observed the caring way in which he treated his widowed mother. He was affectionate and funny with Julie and made us both laugh. He told me early on that he loved me. I felt prized, something I never had felt before. I had the new and delightful feeling of being wanted as much as I wanted him. So when he asked me to marry him that summer of '83, once more I said yes (and damn the consequences). We married in January, 1984. Soon after, Ben officially adopted Julie, who was already calling him "daddy." My father, already carrying around an oxygen tank because of his COPD, attended the small wedding and pronounced me to be "in good hands." Both Scorpios, my father and Ben immediately liked and seemed to understand each other. My father would die a year later, but lived long enough to hold Rebecca right after she was born.

Ben and I both had doubts about the ease of maintaining a long-distance marriage, which ours would certainly be, at least until he received his MFA from Iowa. But by that time I saw myself as so independent that I didn't think it would be a problem. However, as Ben got his degree, a permanent teaching position, then higher and higher administrative positions, it did become a problem—at least for me. I saw him as climbing higher and higher in his profession while, after a few years of teaching the same courses over and over, I was becoming bored at work, stuck at the same level. I had stayed beyond my three-year contract and was told at the end of '84 that I could begin to build a dossier toward indefinite appointment (the equivalent of tenure for us second-class academic staff members). If I chose to do so, I would come up for "review" in 1987. I had mixed feelings, as usual. It was nice to have the security offered by such an indefinite position, but I had always looked upon the job as a temporary stop-gap before my "real work" would begin. I had been teaching only various levels of freshman composition for four years, and longed to teach courses in literature and poetry. Nevertheless, I set about building a file for indefinite appointment, but I was not enthusiastic about it.

After the birth of Rebecca, ten months after we married, I thought that I might be a better counselor than I was a teacher, so at night for several years, I took enough courses to qualify for an MSW in counseling. I enjoyed my internship at a local counseling center, but by that time realized that it would be years before I could accumulate enough hours to begin making a living as a counselor. In addition, because of my own anxiety issues, I felt my stomach clench every time I walked into a room to meet a new client. Deep down, I doubted my ability to "fix" other people's problems, something I now realize that I was never required to do in the six short weeks we were allowed to work with them. So I gave it up, packed away my certificate as "most promising counseling intern" and turned my work energies, once again, to teaching the four levels of English composition I was hired to help create and to teach.

* * *

From the center of the tedium of teaching the "same old classes," I searched, semester after semester, for ways to bring complexity to the teaching, to the process. One resource was the work of the Quaker Parker J. Palmer, who wrote during that time several rather radical books about the art of teaching. For instance, in his book *To Know as We Are Known: Education as a Spiritual Journey (1993),* he writes, "Seldom do we live up to the truth we are given, but that does not mean we must cease speaking the truth. Instead, we must be obedient to the whole of our truth—including our frequent failure to live it out. If we can do that, with ourselves and with each other, the words of truth will continue to be given, and we will be given the power to live them more fully."

Perhaps.

Over the course of 27 years in the department, I attempted new twist after new twist on the material: service-learning courses in which my students learned to "give back" to the communities from which they came; online classes so that my adult students did not always have to make the trek to campus and struggle with child-care and parking. I was "allowed" to teach creative writing once or twice, and a course or two in the honors department, but even then was disappointed by the lack of interest and enthusiasm I seemed to arouse as a teacher. I don't know if my self-assessment is accurate. I believe that, largely an introvert, a part of me has always been uncomfortable being the center of attention at the front of the classroom. Therefore, I tried many ways to teach in a non-teacher-centered way. I felt much more comfortable in my office, having one-on-one conferences with the students who came in. Because I had earned that additional counseling degree in the late 80s, I often found myself counseling students as well as helping them with their writing. In at least one case, I did both. One student wanted to publish a book about how she had been sexually abused as a child. With my help, that did come to pass.

Generally, however, I feared the single inevitable negative comment in the semester's student evaluation packet, and finally gave myself permission to stop reading them at all. I have never regretted it.

Although I did receive "indefinite appointment" after seven years there, and several teaching awards, I always doubted the efficacy of my work for the next twenty. There were few successes to point to, and as I saw my third husband, like my first and second, rise in his profession to all kinds of accolades, I doubted more and more my own skill and talent in my chosen profession. I started to think of teaching as my "day job" while more and more I turned to the piano and poetry to develop my sense of self-esteem in the world of work.

And so, while we were required to sit at our desks for eight hours a day, despite the fact that there was little to do, I would open a new window on my computer and work on my poetry. These lines from the third section ("Uncertainty Principles") from my long poem "Baubo Ponders Questions of Quantum Physics" comforted me when I doubted my own value:

You cannot be measured.
Just when you think
you know who and how big

you are,
you take a quantum leap
to somewhere else

to appear larger
or smaller than you
were.

Never check your watch,
count your money,
gauge your progress.

Don't look under the bed,
assume the worst,
look back.

Burn measuring sticks of all
kinds with their proud
certainties.

Drop-outs and fairy tale
heroines have always
known this. Physicists

in solemn white coats assess,
shake heads, shrug, spread
their large hands.

In the midst of the ongoing changes in our department, a speaker mentioned a 1992 book by Margaret J. Wheatley called *Leadership and the New Science: Discovering Order in a Chaotic World*, which I immediately bought. The fluidity and creativity of the universe it described was exciting; however, at times I found myself feeling overwhelmed with some of the anxiety I felt when I first looked into the heavens on Mt. Palomar—very small, alone, homeless, insignificant. But then there are passage like this, which resonate for me on a very deep level:

I want to move into a universe that I trust so much that I give up playing God.

I want to stop holding things together. I want to experience such safety that the concept of 'allowing'—trusting that the appropriate forms can emerge—ceases to be scary. I want to surrender my care of the universe and become a participating member, with everyone I work with, in an organization that moves gracefully with its environment, trusting in the unfolding dance of order.

I write, "Yes! What is this, but the Tao?"

About her students, Wheatley writes, "They wanted to get organized at the start; I wanted them to move into confusion. I urged them to create more information than they could possibly handle. I guaranteed them that at some point the information would self-organize in them, crystallizing into interesting forms and ideas." In my journal I note, as if answering her, "Good advice for writers. And this feels like what is happening to me, but maybe the crystal-creating moment isn't here yet. There is a role of time, it seems, in all this."

As I write this, over twenty years later, I find myself in this very process. I am re-reading all twenty-five volumes of my messy journals and trusting that something—a new story—a different perspective—will take form in the doing. It is indeed like a late-life pregnancy: creation does not come on our terms, but we nevertheless can create an opening for what seems to want to be born. Wheatley makes the analogy to our lives: how it is only by looking back, gaining perspective, that we see the shape that gives our life meaning (as in the Jimmy Stewart movie "It's a Wonderful Life"—a classic holiday movie for our family). I guess we have to trust that, in the middle of all the endless detail that seems at odds with the Great Plans we once had for our lives, there is a dance being danced, hopefully one of balance, grace, and joy.

For many years I had believed that life would not "give" me what I really wanted: a perfect grade. I had dreams for many years of going through other people's houses and backyards, taking "short-cuts" to my own home. I was trying to get "mine" by invading other people's space. I would cheat in small ways, certain that life would not look out for my best interests. For instance, if a clerk would accidentally give me back more change than was warranted by the purchase, I would not tell her, pocketing the extra as my "due."

One night I had a dream: I was in a department store and wanted a sun hat but I had no money, so I was going to steal it—shoplift it—sneak out of the store without paying. Just as I got to the checkout counter, a beautiful black woman, another customer, turned around and smiled and offered to buy the hat for me. Somewhat disgruntled at being found out, I "allowed" her to buy the hat for me, then left the store. Shortly, she came out and also gave me a single mattress, which I attached to my car. I heard someone say that the store stayed open late just for her because she was such a good customer.

Gradually it became clear to me that this beautiful black woman (Jung might call her the "good mother") was the life force/the universe herself, in a form not usually associated with wealth or power, but who, if allowed, would furnish me with all my needs, including, as symbolized by the single bed, an inner independence that comes from trusting the twisting, unpredictable process of life. No longer would I need to "trespass" or steal or manipulate to get where I thought I needed to go. I began (in short spurts, but still) to trust life to "take me home."

I think my mother would have been pleased, if she could have moved beyond our different symbols and metaphors. In Matthew 6: 25-34, Jesus says, "Therefore I say unto you, Be not anxious for your life, what ye shall eat, or what ye shall drink; nor yet for your body, what ye shall put on. Is not the life more than the food, and the body than the raiment? Behold the birds of heaven, that they sow not, neither do they reap, nor father into barns; and your heavenly Father feedeth them...Consider the lilies of the field, how they grow; they toil not, neither do they spin; yet I say unto you, that even Solomon in all his glory was not arrayed like one of these."

Still, I would never consider myself Christian, nor indeed, accept any label meant to define or limit my spiritual self. And I'm pretty sure that Jesus didn't have an anxiety disorder.

So in 2017 I finally took my own advice in that part of my poem called "Uncertainty Principle": I threw out all my students' gradebooks as well as their notes of gratitude, which I know I will never re-read, and all of their evaluations of me—good or bad—which I was always afraid to look at in the first place. Now I would never have to apply a "fix" on what kind of teacher I had been.

Tying the Knot

I struggle, spread on the bow, sweat
dripping to wet fingerless gloves,

to tie a bowline in the stiff
slimed hulking rope of the mooring.

Patiently you have told me: "out
of the hole, round the tree, into

the hole" but line resists loop, hole
laps backwards or rabbit

runs round the tree widdershins
and under my hands falls away

to nothing. Neither has my double
hitch held, the second twist

taking a wrong turn, sliding
free, unsnagged, deep

into churning water. You've tried
to show me how to plait the figure

eight, infinite knot holding
firm under stress but in calm,

slipping free. I've shrunk from the bright
beam of love's dazzling ring,

that lasso's unwavering light.
I've shied from enclosure, cheered when

the cowpoke's lariat falls
flat. Yet how tenderly

you would wrap a tasseled cord
round the skittish bones of my wrist

then your own as we'd lace
vows; you'd lead me, blindfolded

mare from a blazing barn,
lash me like that other sailor

to a mast of trust. Show me,
my Houdini, once again

how to tie that automatic
knot, how bitter ends

come naturally to connection,
how blunt, blind fingers find

the way to links that simply last
or loosen on command, even

in the dark of inattention,
even under water, even

in a sunken trunk bound with
leather straps, even as,

expert, lithe, adept, we brim
with, hold each other's breath.

Teach me that.

Nine:

Old Camping Gear

The story whispered around me as a teenager by
indiscreet relatives was that I was conceived in June,
1944, under the stars, on a camp bed by the Rattlesnake
River near Stafford, Kansas. Even with that background,
however, as a girl in Kansas, I had never liked camping (my
only experience having been fighting off the giant
grasshoppers in Girl Scout Day Camp) until my second
husband, Jamie, showed me what living in nature for short
periods of time was like. We traveled to and from California
several times in our little VW with our modest camping gear.
Once we camped for a week in Chama, New Mexico. We
sunbathed nude in the "high country" where I developed a
painful case of sun poisoning on my feet. Although I enjoyed
lying in the sun (without sunscreen), smelling the piñon pines,
watching the clouds gather in the west and glide smoothly to
the east during the day, I wondered to myself, pounding tent
stakes in the cold rain under a boulder in the Chama River

Gorge, getting our water from the hopefully clean stream, shivering by the fire while trying to keep warm, if there were not gender differences regarding the propensity to adventure. I would not have been camping rough if it hadn't been for Jamie. I asked him about it, as well as his desire to take LSD out there in the wilderness, far away from help if it became needed. He said that it was his nature to "explore the other side of the mountain." Yeah, well, it's not always mine, especially when it's dangerous and uncomfortable. Jesus, it was cold.

* * *

So when he left me and Julie, asking blithely for our sleeping bags "because Jill and I could use them," I found myself in the position of wanting to continue camping on my own, in my own way. Of course I wasn't on my own: Julie and our dog, Rena, were with me. We needed new equipment. So again with the help of my father, I accumulated a small tent (which I upgraded as I had more daughters); a small butane stove with one burner; new sleeping bags and pads (which I also upgraded as my bones became sharper); water carrier; coffee maker and other simple camping cooking gear.

Every summer, usually in early August when my summer-school teaching ended, we (usually one of our three daughters at a time) would pack up and head 40 miles north to a beautiful state park with isolated camping spots on Lake Michigan. It was an opportunity, not only for me to reconnect with nature in a way I rarely had the opportunity to do in the city, but also for me to dive deep into the lives of my individual daughters: Julie, and later Rebecca and Laney. Sadly, this was something my mother would never even have thought herself capable of doing for the two of us. Fortunately or unfortunately, Ben, my third husband, never liked to camp, having had enough "bivouacking" (as he called it) in the Army, so he never wanted to come with us. So, in the midst of the three-ring circus which was our family in the late '80s and '90s, the carefully-scheduled few summer days alone with each girl were very important to me.

As she grew into adolescence, Julie led me through a series of teen magazine identity-revealing quizzes while camping. She was at that intense stage of discovering who she was and who she wasn't. (As I took the quizzes right along with her, I found that there were aspects of myself that I might do well to become better acquainted with!) She was spreading her wings in all sorts of ways, displaying surprising insights and maturity. But then there were still moments, though less often, when she was tired or nervous that I found it difficult to get along with her. Too often I lost it and got mad. But all was well when we lay on the beach for three hours in the afternoon and read trashy novels, though at night she woke me up whenever I snored!

When it was Rebecca's turn, we read aloud the Laura Ingalls Wilder books (we had each read them several times). Every time I came to the part in which their dog died, I couldn't finish without breaking down. We both sobbed. Becca had begun to make baby clothes for her own American Girl doll of that era, whom she had brought along. During the day, I pushed Rebecca in the inner tube against strong waves, we found beautiful stones, practiced riding our bikes 'no hands,' stuffed ourselves on hot dogs and s'mores and had good sound sleeps. She helped me set up tent and camp—we both liked doing that, I think. A pre-teen, she had started bathing and washing her hair more frequently—even in the rudimentary shower setup in camp—a sure sign of pre-adolescence. It was 1994, and she was almost 10.

Laney started all-day kindergarten that year and, demonstrating her growing independence, left her stuffed animal Patch on the front porch instead of taking it with her as she had done the previous year. She was growing a bit more rebellious and outspoken, yet had apparently comforted some of the smaller children on the first day of school. Laney and I also had a great day at the beach, nature center, and playground between a few gentle rain showers. She kept waking up at night because it was so dark! Yet she seemed to relish summer sensuousness—reading while walking with a loose tooth sticking out. The summer she turned seven, she wrote this poem while camping, one of her first:

A little feather
sits all alone
on the beach
in my reach
in the sand
like no band
like no stone
all alone
right by me!

One year, Rebecca wanted to get a new notebook because she had a sudden inspiration for a story but nothing to write on. We drove to the nearest Walgreens to buy the necessary supplies and then both wrote by flashlight, hunched over in our tent. We also biked, visited Goodwill, went to the Nature Center. Laney and I did similar activities, the water often too cold—even in August—for swimming. Laney cussed out all the gnats and flies harassing us.

There was such a sweetness and sadness at being there with just one girl, deep gratitude for the close companionship of a loved child in the heart of nature. No matter the year, it always helped to take each girl camping separately for at least one night to remind me of what we both missed when the needs of the rest of the family intruded. But I always had a huge lump in my throat while driving one back to collect another. I thought being there longer with each girl would help, but it didn't because each year's camping site was so overlaid with memories of the other two. It was hard to feel just the sweetness without the accompanying sadness of their growing up.

As in sailing, which I started to learn in my late 50s, camping demands not only accommodations to weather, but also to the ages and personalities of the participants. One year, because of lousy weather, Rebecca and I spent a lot of our time in Sheboygan exploring the shops and getting "makeovers" at the department store. She introduced me to filling-station, one-dollar cappuccinos, and we used the "self-timer" on my 35 mm camera to take "selfies" (before that was even a word) of the two of us. At thirteen—almost fourteen—Becca didn't seem to like the outdoors as much as she used to, probably because of all the bugs. Mainly, we read. Thirteen—almost fourteen—is a hard age to be, for both girl *and* mother. Often we ended up playing cards. I taught her gin rummy and bridge. Once I stopped trying to get her to do what I *thought* we should be doing (reveling in nature), I think she had some fun. I did, anyway.

When it was Julie's turn, then about 20, she was just back from a trip to Berkeley and spent a lot of time talking about relationships and nature. Around the campfire she pointed to the example of trees—how they take in CO_2 and transform it to oxygen. Her point was that they work a kind of Buddhist transformation—taking in the negative, transforming it, and putting forth positives of humor and joy. A 'houseless person,' as they were called in Berkeley, told Julie that she was an 'old soul.' I wasn't surprised. Actually, I've been told that too (I think it's a come-on, personally), but my response has always been, 'Well then, you'd think I'd have learned more by now, wouldn't you?'

Julie needed to talk about her homesickness for Oberlin, where she went to college, and her insecurity about her next step in life. I remember when she was 14 (like Rebecca), things seemed so much simpler and her wishes so much more easily met, though it didn't seem so at the time. The days of silliness seemed over and adult earnestness was on the horizon. I didn't know my role in all this and felt frustrated and sometimes impatient. I know that all lasting relationships constantly have to be redefined and reinvented, but it isn't easy and I don't always like it.

Laney wanted to go last that year, probably so that we could go home together. We shopped for all her school supplies in Sheboygan, then had dinner by the campfire. During her two days, we biked, but, not surprisingly, had different ideas about where we wanted to go. I liked long level rides along country roads flanked by wildflowers. She preferred the up-and-down loops of the campground roads. We did a little of each. She spent a long time learning how to skip stones (she picked it up quickly). She chose a poster of the spotted white owl at the nature center for her room. She skipped stones while telling me a story of a man who was warned that, if his stone sank, he would die; if it didn't, he would live forever. She said that maybe she could get so good skipping stones that she would live forever. The waves were pretty big so I helped her to maneuver the inner tube before she rode the waves to shore, over and over again. I accidentally (well sort of) dunked her and so we had to go back to the shower house to wash the sand out of her hair. Then I sat in front of our fire while Laney returned from a bike ride (me too tired to go).

The next summer Rebecca wanted us all to go camping together for a shorter time. While that would perhaps have eliminated some of my sadness at leaving two daughters behind, it would also have diluted the precious time I had with each of my special daughters, so I said no.

* * *

Suddenly, our daughters were all out of childhood. Laney was twelve: She was pulling away, naturally, I guess, but I no longer had a little girl. She had first turn at our camp site that year, but she got mad and didn't speak to me because I wouldn't play bridge with her RIGHT NOW. I hoped she would get over it soon because it was fun being with her. I wasn't sure whether I should let her work through her own bad temper or try to be the peace maker. But the short time we had together suggested that perhaps I should be the one to bridge our gap. It was hard for me to remember she was only twelve, demanding, for instance, that I drive her and her friend to Montana to see the Indigo Girls, to which I had just taken them earlier in the summer when that singing group had been in Milwaukee. Sometimes she seemed much older, and sometimes I forgot that she was no longer a little girl. Eventually she admitted to feeling disappointed at not being able to do everything she wanted to do with me. She had looked forward to family time this summer, but there hadn't been much. Ben was working, Julie hadn't been there, Rebecca had her own projects, and I was always sailing or working with my door shut as if, to use her words, 'I didn't have any children.' Feeling immensely guilty, I tried to explain why sailing and writing were so important to me right then, and I thought she understood, as much as a twelve-year-old can understand a fifty-five-year-old, but it was clear that I had been insensitive to her needs. I had seen her playing cards in her room alone that summer, listening to music and just let her be, glad that there wasn't another demand on my time. How short-sighted.

Or was it?

Camping, we played two-handed bridge, trying to let it build a bridge between us. It was hard to know how to deal with conflict in an area where it had never existed before. And then I had to take her back just as we had begun to rebuild a tentative connection.

Rebecca was increasingly busy with her teenage life, volunteering at the emergency room in light of her desire (at that time) to become a pediatrician. She practiced with her cross-country team, for which I took my turn making what seemed like endless pans of lasagna. We still had a good time camping together as long as we stayed as far away from bugs as possible. This often meant shining flashlights into every single corner of our zipped-up tent before bedtime. The many innocuous daddy-long-legs had to be caught in cups and thrown outside—quickly—before the tent was zipped up again! One night we forgot to lock up the Cinnamon Toast Crunch and were awakened by a pair of raccoons finishing up the box! During the days, we biked and ran and drove around the countryside, naming the horses we saw after current members of the English royalty, then having fun getting "lost" before we, in no hurry for once, found our way back.

Julie was living away from home in her first serious relationship and with her first full-time job, which involved dealing with a somewhat tyrannical boss. Turning more and more toward her interest in the environment, she despaired about the state of the world. Yet she still came camping with me. We walked along the north dunes boardwalk one early evening and saw hundreds and hundreds of huge green dragonflies swarming, trying to fly into the strong west wind. They must have been four inches long. In the waning sun, I watched them glisten while I heard Julie scold four eleven-year-old girls for sliding down the fragile dunes.

In response to her despair over the way the world was going, I tried to reaffirm the place to which I still need constantly to return. Giving up insures failure. One must embrace neither blind faith nor hopelessness but be open to those opportunities that do show themselves to make the world a better place. Perseverance is necessary. I must keep on writing and returning to the piano, to all my jobs and "callings" even if I am often disappointed with the results: do my best, admit mistakes, and keep going on. We must be what we are, and the end result is not ours to see. It would be arrogant to assume what the future holds, and usually only our fear and pride pretend to know what's in store for us. But these things have to be learned through experience, and I suspect that what was meant to be comforting was heard as naiveté or indifference by my twenty-two-year-old daughter. But camping gave us the time to talk about what was most important to both of us. I found that sharing my thoughts with my daughters, one on one, was a great and unexpected pleasure, despite our differences in age.

* * *

I loved the deliberateness of camping—everything had to slow down; nothing could be rushed or sloppily done. Water had to be carried; firewood had to be fetched; precautions taken. I loved walking on the beach in the evening, eyes following a dandelion seed taking its own sweet time parachuting over the water before it even thought of touching down. I loved watching the busy, raucous, daytime seagulls gather together and fly silently east far out over Lake Michigan to sleep on the gentle swells. And I loved making fires with just matches and a little kindling, feeling ridiculously proud when I had a nice, banked fire going for s'mores, or just to gaze into as long as I wanted. And when I left the tent in the middle of the night to pee, I loved looking up at the stars, so many more than we could see in the city. I always wished that our life "back home" could be as mindful and unhurried, but of course it never was.

Sometimes when it rained I wanted one of those cute little campers which you can pull behind your car and raise the canvas when you arrive, but I never even rented one. Somehow that would have meant a departure from actually lying down on the earth (though I welcomed a sewn-in floor and zippered door). Dirt, insects, the threat of rain were all part of the process, and living in an aluminum camper would never have been the same.

I would like to go camping again. Someday. If it weren't too cold or rainy and if someone else would put up the tent, and if the human form of the Lyme disease vaccine is ever approved. But while continuing to declutter our house, I doubt that anyone will want all this forty-year-old camping gear, quite primitive by today's standards. Yet I can't quite make myself throw it out.

My parents never threw out their moldy canvas camp bed either.

Three Days at Lake Michigan, August, 1994

i. Rebecca's Trust

Looking out at what is so much
greater than ourselves,
you rush toward waves,
letting them break
over and over,
over your
delight.

Floating on your back,
you see that there is nothing between
you and the great emptiness above.
You watch a gull turn
sideways, disappear.
Later, reaching for pebbles
lapped by shallows,
discovering color
and location to be mere
illusions of watery light,
you pluck a perfect
green stone.

Gathering a great mound of sand,
you place the unblinking oval of rock
near the tip.
"This is for trust,"
you pronounce, not even
glancing back
as you set the watch.

ii. Julie's Dream

I find the opal
bone of a gull
while you sleep.

Last year you
would have combed
beach grass with me but

this year you sleep,
exhausted by growing up,
on the warmth

of the sand, swaddled,
lullaby'd by billows
of water and air.

Your breath comes
even, slow, your
relaxation absolute,

lying there,
dreaming the treasure of
yourself, being borne

by the beach
on a small
square of blanket.

Now it comes
to me that
my labor is complete,

that I never really
had to labor.
All that is required

is to relinquish
my need and to behold
this perfect

vision of you,
safe, loved, and breathed
by what first
delivered me you.

iii. Laney on the Edge

We play at the edge
all day,
the last day,
come to the beach
still bearing the hollow
where yesterday your sister
slept, and the hill where, day before,
your other sister set a watch.

Not ready yet to risk
the swells,
not yet too tired,
you trifle at the edge,
writing your name and mine
on the sandy slate,
tempting watery erasers,
which advance,
again and again.

You make a village
of rocks I fetch for you
to be buried like toes
under sand, safe
from disaster.

You are discovering
how easily
things melt away.
You assemble shelter
around what you find
beautiful.

Cupping my face, you tell me not
to grow old, that my gray
hair troubles you.

"Have you forgotten when I was a baby?"
you ask.

"Always remember it,"
you charge, slipping away.

And I do remember, and I
have also forgotten.

In the middle of the buried village
I set a branch of cottonwood and
a stick with arms and legs:
scarecrows.

This hoarded, hidden harvest
is not to be plundered.

On the edge
we hold hands and fly
through flocks of resting gulls.

Our footprints
grow lighter,
more
delicate.

Like birds,
they rise,
disappear,
alight again.

Ten:

"The Shadow" and Blue Moons

Growing up in a nation founded by Puritans, one must continue to try to correct/purify oneself every day, it appears, in all aspects of one's life. In the 1990s, for me, those areas were work and relationships. The idea of progress in both seemed of utmost importance. Therefore, when two important books on these topics came out in the same year, 1996, I had trouble with the basic assumptions of both the Jungian psychologist James Hillman's *The Soul's Code: In Search of Character and Calling* and Deepak Chopra's *Path to Love,* respectively. The main stumbling block I had with both authors was their insistence upon acceptance of the Self's 'dark' side. In middle age this was hard for me. I thought that maybe I had misunderstood what they meant by 'acceptance.' Acknowledgement—yes; acceptance was another thing. I didn't know; probably I was 'addicted' to perfection. I suspected I still had a number of fixed ideas that required letting go of—and the fear that accompanies such letting go.

Today, in early old age, that fear has mostly dropped away. I believe that I do accept what Carl Jung, anyway, termed the "dark side"—the unintegrated parts of one's personality, which we first often see as "dark" or "bad" or even "evil." According to Jung,

> *Beneath the social mask we wear every day, we have a hidden shadow side: an impulsive, wounded, sad, or isolated part that we generally try to ignore. The Shadow can be a source of emotional richness and vitality, and acknowledging it can be a pathway to healing and an authentic life. We meet our dark side, accept it for what it is, and we learn to use its powerful energies in productive ways. The Shadow knows why good people sometimes do 'bad' things. Romancing the Shadow and learning to read the messages it encodes in daily life can deepen your consciousness, imagination, and mind (from* Romancing the Shadow *by Connie Zwieg and Ben Wolf, 1958).*

Two different therapists, twenty years apart, have asserted that my "shadow" is Powerlessness, which needs to be integrated in order for me to be whole. This has always seemed hard because, to me, "Powerless" is what women have always been, despite the second wave of feminism, through which I had lived. My mother was certainly Powerless.

Looking back to early 1997, when Julie first left home for college, it was hard to see her go. Nevertheless, she seemed to be developing a wisdom about relationships that I hadn't even begun to develop until my 30s. She put it so well: her 'higher' Self seemed to be growing by leaps and bounds while her 'ego' trotted along on the ground trying to keep up. Wish I'd said that! When I quoted her to Ben, he said, 'Did you tell her it's always like that?'

Ben himself was having trouble sleeping—was worried about money, his mother, his brother, and his work, the possibility of a new job. We both hated not being in control, though these issues exhibited differently in each of us: through fear (me) or through anger (Ben). I dreamed that he and I participated in a strange but beautiful sort of square dance. We separated and came together, repeatedly, over and over.

My job seemed especially stale in the new semester, but I tried to put that feeling aside each time I walked in to a classroom or talked with a student. I believed that if I watched for the unexpected, I could perhaps slip between the frames of routine to explore new, unfamiliar depths, like finding an unexpected door to a new room in one's dreams.

Rebecca asked me to teach her about the Tarot. She was only eleven, but we made a start, doing a three-card spread on her change of interest from theater to ballet. Like all my daughters, she seems to have a strong visual/intuitive/poetic streak, so she was immediately able to see some of the connections. She seemed open. . . and of course that's what is necessary.

About the same time, I dreamed of an old, out-of-tune piano, which made me wonder what I needed to do to get back "into tune." I had an image of something moving, flowing— something like an amoeba. It was held back for a time by a kind of cardboard template glued to it, to which it had to conform. But once that template was removed, torn away, the amoeba was once more free to move as it would, more naturally. That was as close as I could come to an image of how it might free up possibilities if I got rid of old templates, patterns, measuring devices, to allow a less clear-cut, but perhaps more 'natural,' pattern for my life to evolve into, even if it didn't at first seem obvious.

* * *

One day a colleague put a clipping from the school newspaper in my mailbox. It featured one of my former students, a black basketball player named Cyrus, who named me as "his favorite teacher" and listed his "dream" as making the NBA, but his "goal" as becoming an elementary school teacher. I think I was perhaps somewhat helpful in keeping Cyrus from dropping out his freshman year. I worked with him partly because I saw something special about him from the first day of the lowest remedial class. Two years later, he had passed the stringent second-semester 'regular' English class and was flourishing. There was appreciation there, of a kind. Small, but there.

Always, there seemed to be a connection between the challenges to my students and those to myself: there was often such a gap between what was expected of them and what they could actually do, that even the attempt to teach sometimes seemed a more or less meaningless activity. Of course I could and did say the same of myself—the same sad gap between what I expected of myself and what I could actually accomplish. It is hard to trust progress we can't see evidence of when we think we need to see it. So: acceptance of present 'reality' without giving up the goal was the same paradox I kept stumbling back upon. I asked myself what I'd learned in my 28 years of teaching, and answered: "What have I learned? Meet students only halfway; the work has to be theirs; it's OK to fail—sometimes that's the only place the learning can take place; don't try to be a 'good teacher'—just teach." I noted in my journal that chaos theory reinforced the unlikely idea that, at certain unstable points in the life of a system, an infinitesimal influence can have a momentous effect.

During some of my "free time" at work, I read a 1989 book by physicists John Briggs and F. David Peat called *Turbulent Mirror: An Illustrated Guide to Chaos Theory and the Science of Wholeness.* In it, they use a poem by Richard Wilbur, "The Writer," to demonstrate the fractal nature of poetry: i.e. "each part is a symbol of, or repeats the theme of the whole. Poetry is an interlocking series of metaphors, or rather, 'reflectaphors.' " They go on to write, "Fractals are both order and chaos. They have self-similarity at different scales, but this self-similarity is not self-sameness and is unpredictable and random. The tension between similarities and differences in reflectaphors also creates for us . . . a sense that what we're experiencing is organic, is both familiar and unknown."

In the "Forward" to their book, they quote the Jungian Joseph Campbell:

When you reach an advanced age and look back over your lifetime, it can seem to have had a consistent order and plan, as though composed by some novelist. Events that when they occurred had seemed accidental and of little moment turn out to have been indispensable factors in the compositions of a consistent plot. So who composed that plot? . . . Your whole life is composed by the will within you. And just as people whom you will have met apparently by mere chance became leading agents in the structuring of your life, so, too, will you have served, unknowingly, as an agent giving meaning to the lives of others. The whole thing gears together like one big symphony with everything unconsciously structuring everything else. . . . It is even as though there were a single intention behind it all, which makes some kind of sense, though none of us knows what the sense might be, or has lived the life that he [sic] intended.

I thought to myself: *This* is the kind of stuff I wanted to be teaching, and not being able to do so was probably one of the reasons I felt my 'real' teaching flagging.

Nevertheless, my being given permission to develop the new partly online course in creative writing was an example of taking advantage of an unstable system. At such times of instability, says chaos theory, small influences can have huge effects. I didn't know how 'huge' an effect this course would ever have, but I was pretty sure I would never have had that opportunity several years before, when the departmental 'system' was more stable. The need for chaos, for the trickster, for disorder has always resonated with me. I suppose this is obvious in many aspects of my life—from three marriages to

124

my messy drawers and desktops. I need a 'rich soup' for the creativity of new insights.

I think about the concept of "gift": that, in at least one book of fairy tales, gifts are given almost always by magical creatures, and usually a) in a time of great need or passage, or b) in exchange for previous good deeds. Or both. Often both. In some cases the 'gift' is not 'given' at all, but stolen by some enterprising youth (usually) from the magical creature. Often, in fairy tales anyway, this kind of stealing is OK—sometimes even necessary and in some sense, expected, as the next step of growth: gifts as enlargements of the world—of possibility.

* * *

I read May Sarton's most recent journal, *Eighty-Two*, which takes her up to a year before her death in the summer of '95. It was very sad to read, for several reasons. First, she was so frail, so weak, so ill and yet continued to struggle on alone (though she had some paid help and many, many friends). But more so, she became extremely depressed, even obsessed with the idea that she had never been really accepted by American critics—by the canon of academia in America. She beat herself over the head with this; it seemed to eat her alive. She valued the increasingly large sale of her books, the letters from all the 'ordinary' people who loved her work, but couldn't rest content with that. She worried about what her biographer would say. Apparently some male critic had written very harsh reviews of her work in the 50s and 60s. She seemed never to get over it though she kept on writing and publishing.

Of course, her life resonated with mine as well. Despite my bravado about losing the poetry contests I had repeatedly entered, the anticipation of failure or success interfered with any current writing I might have been doing. I reminded myself that in some cultures, the true artist leaves no trace and doesn't sign the work, even in some cases, as in sand painting, destroys the work. But in *our* culture, as Lewis Hyde and others have pointed out, art is a commodity and its worth and the worth of its creator are judged thereby. And women writers/artists have been anonymous *long enough*—why should we seek such anonymity again? Angela, still alive at that time, applauded.

It didn't help to ask an established female professor in the English department, and the author of several well-received books of poetry, for "advice" planning my creative writing course. Neither did it help to discover that she had long been *judging* entries for a contest like the ones I had just *entered*. Older than she by several years, I came home to find one of my contest manuscripts rejected along with a handful of poems from another source. So my ego had come out in full force and was trampled.

A work colleague, who left AOC to train as a Unitarian minister, left me her copy of *Rilke's Letters to a Young Poet*, which I re-read. In his early thirties, Rilke would write his famous admonition: "Be patient toward all that is unresolved in your heart and try to love the questions themselves." I think that this would be a great epigraph for anyone's journal. Rilke advises his correspondent "not to look outward for validation—magazines, critics, the like"—but "to look only within and ask whether or not one would die if s/he couldn't write." I'd always thought that a bit extreme; however, it is true that life would seem much less meaningful were I not to write in my journal, where I have received so many insights, or write poetry, when I'm riding a tremendously exciting wave that carries me further than I have gone before. No—I wouldn't want to live without that.

Looking up a quotation by T.S. Eliot for Rebecca one evening, I started to re-read the "Four Quartets" and was amazed (as usual) at how much more I related to them than I had thirty years ago. When I read this passage from "East Coker," I started to cry:

So here I am, in the middle way, having had twenty
> *years—*
Twenty years largely waste, the years of l'entre deux
> guerres—
Trying to learn to use words, and every attempt
Is a wholly new start, and a different kind of failure
Because one has only learnt to get the better of words
For the thing one no longer has to say, or the way in
> *which*
One is no longer disposed to say it. And so each venture
Is a new beginning, a raid on the inarticulate
With shabby equipment always deteriorating
In the general mess of imprecision of feeling
Undisciplined squads of emotion. And what there is to
> *conquer*
By strength and submission, has already been discovered
Once or twice, or several times, by men whom one cannot
> *hope*
> *To emulate—but there is no competition—*
There is only the fight to recover what has been lost
And found and lost again and again: and now, under
> *conditions*
That seem unpropitious. But perhaps neither gain nor
> *loss.*
For us, there is only the trying. The rest is not our
> *business.*

I was amazed that even T.S. Eliot, often considered the
best English-speaking poet of the 20th century, had once felt
such lack of self-confidence. I was also struck by the way he
used such a long line, which seems, on the surface, to be so
prosy and yet is so moving that it can make one weep. And
that, I thought, comes from the quality of his life—not the
personal details, maybe—but the quality of his mind that
allowed the truth of what he was saying to come through, not
blocked by self-importance or self-pity (which are ultimately
the same thing). Today, I relate that to what the poet Jane

Hirshfield, in her 2015 book of essays, *Ten Windows: How Great Poems Transform the World*, writes: "poetry is never purely description, it is a portrait of a state of being, of soul."

A dream from about that time also helped. I kept wanting a new mixing bowl, but every time I got a new aluminum one, it would start to turn dark as soon as I put anything into it. So I realized that what I needed was a new copper bowl which would retain its own integrity/nature and would not react with whatever it held. Copper can become tarnished but can always be cleaned and polished back to its original brightness. And copper is the metal associated with the Great Goddess. The imagery seemed to suggest that the ego is like an aluminum bowl, reacting to whatever is put inside, whereas the deeper self is unchanged by whatever "happens" to it.

One night I also dreamt of having my portrait taken and having my eyes examined at the same time. My dreams often have a wry sense of humor.

Sarton was a good writer and a really fine poet. On the other hand, her philosophical and political ideas now seem somewhat superficial to me despite her obviously knowing much about wrestling with her own demons. I mourned her death as she recounted her journey toward it. We still seem to lack a true, facilitating belief in the possibility of a healthy old age. So many older people are not healthy. We still need models. If we can see that it's possible, not as a rare exception, but really possible, then perhaps more of us could do it.

My old mentor, Ben Spencer, also died that spring. It was he who had taught me to love poetry. He introduced me to Whitman and Dickinson. He used to hold advanced classes at his home, evenings, as we all drank spicy tea. I thought it would be wonderful to be a teacher like he was, and so in 1963 I began the long trek to where I was in the late 90s. Could my current teaching, the job I then held, continue to keep me growing for the next 15 years? I felt such a disconnect between how Dr. Spencer had taught and how I was teaching; it never occurred to me to think about how the times in which we lived had affected our different teaching opportunities.

* * *

Deepak Chopra writes (perhaps too glibly) about the "depths" needed for insight and healing, where anything "becomes possible." He admits that this state is rare, and is perhaps simply a "gift." I found his belief intensely frustrating—an unreachable "heaven" for which only the "elect" are pre-ordained (something like a Puritan view). But instead of a height, I saw it as a depth at which we clearly see our interconnecting roots. I started to think more about Persephone. How do I "get there," I wondered? My meditations seemed to remain shallow. What was missing? What did I need to do? Practice? Wait? Swallow a pomegranate seed?

But even Persephone could not stay in the richness of the Underworld forever; Demeter (the mother) demanded her presence in the mundane world half of the year. I never thought of Persephone's return to earth as sad, but perhaps it was, once she had tasted the freedom and wealth of the Underworld. And so I began to consider a series of poems about Persephone, this time from her point of view. I had some idea of mixing that with the different, but related, ideas of gift, surrender, and sacrifice, but I wasn't sure it would work. But in a way that's the fun, the adventure, the excitement of any art—to see if it *will* work, and/or how well.

But impatience remained a bugaboo. I was so impatient with nearly everyone, including myself. And yet I saw a wonderful model of patience one Friday evening at Walgreens. Laney and I were in the checkout line behind an old woman who took *forever* to get her coupons out, double-check the prices, open her wallet, find her money, count her money, and finally pay. And through it all, the young female clerk was infinitely patient, calm, and friendly, even though she was obviously waiting. I was so antsy I could hardly *stand it*, let alone just stand still and wait, but ever since I have thought of that young woman's patience as a model and have mentally thanked her for it. Too often, I feel like the slow, dim-witted, bumbling old woman who just wants a little attention, but I am rarely the patient, understanding clerk.

About this same time there were bright spots: my weakest student, Randy, who had a third-grade reading level and (according to many) should not even be in college, had made some small progress through perseverance, but (like me) became impatient and discouraged. I realized that, while encouraging him, telling him that the time required to make progress was not important, I was also speaking to myself. I had a dream in which people were admonished to keep their (literal) shirts on.

Spring break finally came and I took a little of that time to drive out to the country. I started at Lizard Mound, with a cold south wind and the winter barrier still across the road. But there were huge, cacophonous flocks of redwings in the oaks lining the road, and, as I walked in, they flew on ahead of me, from tree to tree, as if leading me in.

Meanwhile, Ben interviewed for a promotion to the vice-president (provost) of a local art college. As part of the interview process, he prepared a speech in which he described himself as "a work in progress." Seeing himself as a work in progress certainly accorded with how I saw myself. And as he spoke of what he had learned as a young teacher about leading (teaching) by following, by being open to the truth that he didn't know all the answers, I realized the generally unspoken, but deep, similarity in our values.

As the semester wound down, I found that one-third of my students had dropped or withdrawn, including one of my favorites—an old friend whom I had taught in English 090 and now for the second time in 112. He came to tell me he was withdrawing for a number of reasons, all of which made sense for him then. On the surface, it looked as if the number of withdrawals pointed to something wrong with my teaching, but I didn't think so. It wasn't obvious to me. In most all cases, the students simply couldn't hack it for one reason or another at that point in their lives.

Nevertheless, I cited to myself this occurrence as one more sign that things in my life were "deteriorating." I knew that structures do have to break down first in order to change (at least sometimes), but it was still hard for me to see what replaces/grows out of youth or physical fertility except becoming an old woman. And this culture still ignores old women, and at worst, finds them ugly and disgusting. And this is what I felt I was becoming: unraveled.

Yet, again, insight came, often while I exercised. We 'progress' or 'train' by choosing to return to effort after having fallen away (usually into inertia, doubt, despair, or simply unconsciousness). This insight, not new, always gave me hope whenever it recurred—hope for my own 'spotty' progress as well as for the infinitesimal evidence of growth in my remaining students.

* * *

I took an extra-long weekend to visit Julie in Oberlin as she was to be in a play. She and a few friends had turned the basement of a local restaurant into a kind of black box through sheer energy and will power, and all of this on their own. I was proud of Julie's growth on many levels. She was so good with people and had a level of emotional maturity I wish I had had at her age. Acting had given her a felt knowledge of moving from the center, the Tao, something which I had no words for and was barely conscious of at her age.

Such observations made me reach beyond my post-midlife regrets about how I'd chosen to live my life. I did believe that the 'creative' can correct past mistakes, wrong choices, if given time and trust. And like grass or flowers that have been stepped on, I knew that my poetry and music had begun to spring back even after years of neglect. And who was to say that my present progress wasn't even faster *because* of having been repressed for so long? I missed my youth, but was perhaps finding compensations: insight and understanding being not the least. But also, I was beginning to see the (faint?)

possibility of stepping out of the cloud of fear, depression, sadness, and self-doubt that seemed to have muffled me for most of my life. What a boon if I could step away from that, or at least learn the way out should it recur!

I had a very comforting dream about a pet owl, which I kept in a box for some reason. Sometimes I took it out. I wasn't afraid of it and I would stroke its breast feathers, which it liked. Then it would start to 'groom' the invisible lice from my hair, cleaning out the parasites I wasn't even aware of. When I awoke, I felt tremendously reassured that the 'wisdom' I was letting more and more out of its 'box' would automatically help to clear away many of the 'mind parasites,' some of them unconscious, which had always plagued me—fear, sadness, doubt.

Ben did indeed get the provost's job. I knew that it would help fulfill some of his needs: to make required changes at the art school and to bring home a larger salary, which would help us out tremendously. And we both went full steam ahead on our individual plans for the future. It was still hard for each of us to communicate about and negotiate our separate desires: to understand if one of us didn't always seem to support the other's ideas with anything short of immediate and full enthusiasm. We both have pretty good judgment, but our individual needs to be in total control of everything sometimes caused problems. And while we both said that the fact that his salary being over twice the amount of mine didn't matter a bit in our decision-making, I know that it did for me, and certainly would have mattered if things were reversed. Actually, Ben and I share a lot of the same temperament. But the male/female thing gave an interesting twist to the basic set-up and to my original wish for an equal relationship.

All this brought me back to the idea that making mistakes leads to growth as does the detachment of the artist, but perhaps only temporarily. Even the 'frame' of art seemed unsustainable in everyday life. Maybe consciousness, awareness, enlightenment, whatever—and I wasn't at all sure that all those were equivalent—can only come and go, flicker on and off as we fall away from and return to that state. And maybe this falling away and returning *is* consciousness (at least as available to us humans), *is* the time and motion associated with life (as we know it). Example: the flickering frames of a motion picture in slow motion allow conscious awareness of the essential, the previously unseen, the significant.

Heavy stuff. Now: where was the poetry in it? And the usefulness for our marriage?

Ben left for Copenhagen on a business trip and for a marathon with an old friend. As we prepared the house for reappraisal, I thought that he and I apparently also needed to re-appraise how we made decisions as a team, a unit. Maybe occasional falling away is necessary in relationship too— where the need to readjust leads us back to a renewed sense of possibility.

In my never-ending search for balance, I joined an advanced tai chi class in which I met a woman named Ellen who was to become my best friend. As my other friendships with women often faded for one reason or another, I was thrilled to find someone new—someone who was about my age, who was an artist, and who had four grown children. She knew about husbands and relationships and was willing to explore them with me in a measured way that Angela had not been.

Ben and I were, with the end of the school year and his return from Copenhagen, slowly but happily finding our way back to each other. Julie returned and found a job, Rebecca looked forward to her every-day ballet lessons, and Laney and I, while she was ill with some virus, watched the Marx brothers, put up a bird feeder she had made, and fertilized the rose bushes. I had time to cultivate my new friendship with Ellen.

Predictably, I had a lot of anxiety when one of my children was ill. On one of my country drives, I stopped by a river, sat on the huge roots of a maple tree growing in the water, and watched seeds drift south, listened to the birds (two mourning doves were chasing each other around, either fighting or mating—sometimes it's hard to tell the difference) and trying to understand why I still reacted with so much fear when one of the kids got sick. (Laney's ear infection hadn't responded very well to the second antibiotic.) The simple explanation was that I was still reacting to my sister's death and the trauma of my parents' helplessness— POWERLESSNESS— in the face of the then-uncontrollable polio virus. The deeper question was *why*? How can it be OK in the grand scheme of things for innocent, beautiful children to suffer and die? And of course they do, every day, and not just because of viruses and bacteria, but also because of abuse. I wasn't sure that 'why' was the right question, and yet it was the one my emotions most wanted an answer to.

The primary impulse of caring parents—to protect and nurture—is continually thwarted. And no doubt that is the lesson: that our children are not ours in any real sense of the term; that, once again, we are not in control, a hard lesson for the heart. I knew I was not as overly protective of my children as my parents were of me, but uncontrollable illness apparently still rang my bell. How many Demeter/Persephone poems, I thought, must I write before it was no longer such an obstruction for me? Many years later, Jane Hirshfield would write in one of her *Ten Windows* essays, "Language Wakes Up in the Morning: On Poetry's Speaking," "The writer is driven, goaded, hounded. A letter Rilke sent to his wife makes his sense of extremity clear: a work of art, he wrote, is the outcome of 'having-been-in-danger.' For Rilke, as for many others, the central goad was transience, finding some way to take in and navigate the unbearable knowledge that life will end."

After a talk with Julie about my personal history, I looked back into my journals of the 70s and thought about whether to destroy some or all of them. Angela destroyed hers, saying that they were only for her and no one else. I thought that mine were probably the same. She destroyed all of hers in a burst of disgust for what she saw as the "ego and libido" of her writing.

134

Yet ultimately I didn't have the heart to destroy what was the external form of my many years of hard inner work. Yes, *work*.

To my belated surprise, relationships also take work, as I was finally learning. Ben and I seemed to be drifting into another cycle of separation—mainly because of the different ways in which we spent our days, because of our unending parental responsibilities, and simply because of the dullness of routine and habit. Ellen said that she prided herself on being the one to bring her and her husband back together at times like that, but I resisted, believing that women should not be the only ones responsible for "husbanding" true intimacy in a marriage.

Julie too was struggling with men—insensitive ones, possessive ones, too "free-spirited" ones. I could relate to her being impatient to find the "right" one. I knew how easy it was to "settle"—for all sorts of reasons other than the "right" ones, whatever they were.

Summer school started. A student wrote me a note letting me know how frustrating the summer's reading was for her. Instead of asking for help, she attacked, saying that such "Difficult books should not be assigned." Sigh. Are we then, as teachers, to renounce the "difficult"?

All learning is *work*.

*   *   *

At home, I had to give up "my office" so that there was a "guest room." It niggled but at the time didn't really bother me, since most of my writing I did in my work office. Nevertheless, I had more than a passing thought about what had happened to 'a room of one's own' in my own home?

Despite that, I found some time around the edges of my teaching to return to poetry. I was drawn once again to Whitman's lines in s. 45 of "Song of Myself":

My rendezvous is appointed, it is certain,
The Lord will be there and wait till I come on perfect
terms,
The great camerado, the lover true for whom I pine will
be there.

The lines resonated deeply with me for many reasons: their certainty, mainly. I wondered what he meant by "on perfect terms" and doubted that he meant "perfection," for I was coming at long last to see that "perfection" was not only impossible, but probably undesirable, if one values growth. Progress is fickle; my work on the piano always comes undone. I played only in odd moments when I had nothing else to do and, as was the case as a child, when no one else wanted to watch TV in the same room. I had almost finished working through the Chopin Preludes but not quite—and the earlier ones began to unravel as I neglected them for the more recent ones. Why wouldn't they just *stay done*, accomplished: permanent and perfectly realized parts of my repertoire? I felt like a magician whose spells were constantly coming apart. And not only in the musical realm. Old lessons about everything, including relationships, have constantly to be relearned, renewed, refreshed, at least dusted off now and then.

My frustration seemed speeded up by my advancing age. Why did time so often seem like a thief? I read Stephen Hawking's *A Brief History of Time: From the Big Bang to Black Holes* (1988), in which he sees the universe as a huge expanding circle with no beginning and no end, yet gets stuck thinking there is no creator. Why need the concept of creation be linear?

Indeed.

I thought again of Marion Woodman's 1982 book, *Addiction to Perfection: The Still Unravished Bride*, which explores from a Jungian standpoint some of the causes of compulsory behaviors such as eating disorders. As summarized on amazon.com, "The need to experience a sacred connection to an energy greater than their own drives people to search for an illusory ideal of perfection." Through her discussion of parenthood, creativity, and body image, Woodman goes on to suggest that "freedom from addiction can be found by discovering the wisdom and power of the feminine principle."

Though I was always committed to the drive for personal excellence, slowly I have had to come to terms with my own imperfections and those of 'life' itself many, many times and, to some extent, in some ways, have made peace with it. But it's always a temporary peace that needs to be renegotiated again and again. The hidden gems in an imperfect world seem to be consciousness (awareness) and compassion. And why are these ultimate goods? Because they lead to expansion and creativity. Whereas a perfect world (or life) stands, like the Garden of Eden, complete in its unchanging, oblivious and indifferent symmetry.

Tai chi teaches that, when you find yourself off center, to simply return. For me this means that, instead of listening to thoughts about my poor "progress," I turn away toward the center, and they do seem to dissipate. But not for long. Not forever.

I re-read Carlos Castaneda's *The Power of Silence* (1987) once again and was struck, this time through, by how he seems to make the path to enlightenment seem a lot less bumpy than it actually seems to be. Ambition and impatience and ego never really go away but continue to skulk in corners even when I'm not looking. The deep, wise self is there but usually masked by daily frustrations: one's self-image, self-importance, and all the doubts, fears, vanity, and impatience attendant thereon. The 'withering away' of such aspects of oneself, despite the many opportunities provided by aging and other losses seems ultimately as idealistic and improbable as the 'withering away of the State' in classic Communist theory. People, at least in our present culture, are just too invested in their individual successes and images.

Of course it's also true that believing something to be impossible tends to keep it that way. And so I keep 'trying': staying open to possibilities that haven't manifested yet, searching/waiting for that open/balanced/neutral state that is said to be the door, the gateway to freedom. Decades ago, there was a sense of intense loneliness sometimes, realizing that there was no one with whom I could really talk about these things, and yet it has generally always been that way with me—is perhaps, in some sense, my fate to explore these questions mostly on my own or through reading. Relationships in which I have shared openly some of these questions have not succeeded any more than those in which I have not. Thus—my journals.

August brought more responsibility at work in addition to finishing the summer session. I had little time to process Angela's death in July of 1997, even as I was facing issues similar to hers. Everyone in the family had the summer 'flu; the weather was unseasonably cool and rainy. Laney was able to go camping with me, but it took an inordinate amount of preparation and cleanup time.

Ben was not only (of course) very involved in his new job but had taken on an *ad hoc* evening teaching job at Marquette. He was making almost all of the family money and essentially making all the financial decisions, and then became surprised and upset if I disagreed. Typically, even in my forties, I still feared talking to men about how I was *really* feeling if that implied possible conflict, so I became cool, distant, and estranged, contributing to the anger, distance, and lack of intimacy that gave me so much pain.

I felt 'needy.' So does it come down to a woman/man thing, I wondered? We were both reacting in typical ways according to gender. And then I thought that this must be my challenge: simply not to give up. I wondered if such a relationship with the constant kinds of intimacy and nurturing I'd always wanted was even possible between a man and woman though I'd never really experienced it with a woman either (except my sister). So was I to lower my expectations?

accept what *was*? settle? The image of Hecate, the Crone, appeared in my Tarot cards one morning. I thought that if I could stay open, perhaps she would lead me past my old fears to a "third way": to a new level of understanding.

On March 31 arrived the second full moon of the month, the second "blue moon" of the year. I was watching it rise while waiting for Laney to come out of the library, when I saw a strange thing: a man who, on his way into the library, turned around three times clockwise—deliberately, for no apparent reason. He probably had obsessive-compulsive disorder, but his 'dance' and that of a squirrel I had also been watching, seemed strangely mysterious in the dusk of the rising moon.

It occurred to me that all our obsessions were strangely beautiful, somehow, within the context of our changing lives, as they came and went. Perhaps I needed to do nothing to free myself from the habits of sadness and fear. Perhaps, turning and turning, eventually their arcs would lose more and more momentum, and I would stand free: unwound for a moment in the stillness, like the stillness between movements of a sonata. Things do not progress in straight lines, I thought to myself.

The Beautiful Unnamed

> *Which is more inexpressible, the beautiful or the terrifying?*
> —-Mary Ruefle
>
> *Death is the mother of beauty, mystical,*
> *Within whose burning bosom we devise*
> *Our earthly mothers waiting, sleeplessly.*—Wallace Stevens

i.
A mother of small children learns to forge
ahead to take the brunt of giant grasshoppers,

to capture inch-long centipedes
between Dixie cups to lob outside,

to pull, then pop ticks from baby scalps
before baby or bloody tick realizes,

to chuck fragile daddy longlegs, apologetically,
from tents containing sleeping children,

to spray small limbs with DEET
against mosquitos that might carry virus,

to lure yellow jackets away from ice cream
to drown in sweetened drink.

A woman whose children are grown learns
to stop time: to watch a water strider

skate on liquid film; to feel a dragonfly's
neon needle stitch her close;

to stare while a lady bug gorges
herself on aphids, freeing buds in the garden

while a caterpillar spins itself
into a gold carapace that,

at least this time, turns clear,
swelling with wet, veined, fragile wings;

to note a bee humming above lovers
lying in soft purple vetch.

ii.
Nine hundred thousand species of insects
have been named; thirty million more

remain nameless (their fecundity reaching
far beyond Adam's span of attention).

Eve would gladly do it: take all
the time in the world to weave each new

name into the gauzy web of consciousness.
Naming calms, connects, comforts. A child,

I remember rocking myself in pain, trying to
soothe my unnamed dis-ease,

hearing the threatening buzz of August locusts,
as my father crouched beside me,

impatient to convince that going to
the doctor would not be the death of me,

though it seemed to me to have been
the obvious cause of my sister's.

When he died, thirty years later,
in the hospital, at the very end,

the boy that he once was
called for his mother (by then many years

gone from cancer), to hold his hand, to sing
his name, perhaps to tell him once again

that he was loved and not to be afraid,
that it was safe to sleep.

iii.
Even grown children give us no
leave to die. And yet we do: shape-

shifting them into orphans who
must face, venture to touch, name

their dread, their beautiful Un-
Named, to sound its unsounded depth,

to stutter its new syllables in
unfathomable tongues: perhaps even,

uneasy humans on this still flowing,
happy earth, to hold out their arms

to claim as theirs what once so terrified.

Eleven:

Two Witches and a Telescope

Despite my current intention to "de-clutter" our large house, there are some small objects that I still need and cannot yet release. One of these is a small figurine that I bought around Halloween a few years ago on a writing retreat in a small town. It is a small green witch (witches have been portrayed as green only since the movie *The Wizard of Oz*, which scared me mightily) with an owl on her shoulder and a map of the sky in her hand, looking through a large telescope and smiling. The owl is wearing glasses.

As I've said, when I was about eleven, my parents and I visited the relatively new Hale telescope at Mt. Palomar.

When we came out, after looking at the dark and gigantic universe, I realized that, indeed, there was no "heaven": only a vast empty Nothingness.

What helped, much later, were books that began to be published in the late 90s: books by Stephen Hawking, Brian Greene's *The Elegant Universe*, Fritjof Capra's *The Web of Life,* etc., which provided a whole different view of the universe. No longer was it a void into which I feared being cast away forever, but an invisible web of intelligent connections, ever being woven and re-woven. Slowly I developed a sense of being in a world of creation and complexity beyond what I could imagine, and yet I could learn, like the little witch, something about it and write about it in my poetry and journals.

I never named this little green witch, but I did name another one, who flies on a broomstick on the top of one of my book cases: Baubo. She was given to me by Selena Fox after my solitary "Crone Quest" a year after my last period had occurred at age 48.

Circle Sanctuary is a beautiful place, tucked as it is into the moraines of south-central Wisconsin. Today, much of it has been tamed into walkable paths, but in late summer of 1994, one still had to make one's own way.

I brought my few pieces of gear and set up camp by myself in a willow grove next to a spring. It was quiet there. A cool breeze blew in the grove, insects hummed, the spring bubbled. Over the course of two days, I had several good talks with Selena, but on the whole, this was a solitary quest. I brought green and white candles to light my way: I had first thought to burn the white candle and then the green for renewal, but it seemed more appropriate, once I was there, to burn the green first, symbolizing youth, which is what seemed to be leaving and what I had yet to mourn. Then perhaps the white could take its place. How fast it burned! How fast life goes, and the years of physical fertility! Feelings of loss had not yet turned into those of freedom, but I sensed that possibility and decided to follow some of Jean Shinoda

Bolen's suggestions from her tape "The Wise Woman Archetype: Menopause as Initiation":

- list the sacred moments of your life
- state what you have learned
- find the humor
- open to new creativity

  and, from Selena (not yet a Crone herself),
- list and mourn the losses
- set goals and directions for the future.

It was so beautiful there, in the willow grove, yet willows, I know, symbolize sadness. My mother transplanted one from our Stafford home to the one in Wichita, and, yes, she also transplanted her sadness. It was a lonely tree—just one—and it sought the only water available to it on the Kansas prairie— our sewer pipes. So periodically the roots had to be cut out of our sewer system, just as the roots of sorrow must be clipped now and then lest they block the flow of life. So I grieved and did not apologize for the apparent paucity of my losses.

I grieved
- the loss of youth
- the loss of fertility
- the loss of the career I had hoped for
- Julie's leaving
- the failures of my first two marriages
- the loss of the cuddling of small children who love me unconditionally and think I can do no wrong
- the apparent difficulty of having a true relationship of equality with a man
- my mother's grief

I believed I needed to let go of
- vanity *(Glamour* magazine and the buying of beautiful clothes)
- pride
- ambition
- summer
- my dream to be a "real" college professor
- my relationship with my mother
- the death of my sister
- not being a better pianist, poet, friend, mother
- my dogs who had died
- being beautiful for such a brief time
- catering to men because of their maleness.

I regretted
- my impatience, which has often cost me the present
- the chance to be Somebody
- my timidity and lack of risk-taking in teaching
- not being more generous with time and money
- not being more outspoken about my beliefs
- not spending more of my youth with Ben.

Sacred moments for me had been
- looking up into Ben's eyes and seeing the love there
- all the preparations surrounding Julie's birth
- finding the feather at an effigy bird mound when I was unsure of my path in life
- camping on Rock Island, sleeping on the beach, walking back the next morning
- camping naked in California
- other moments in nature, esp. with Julie as a child
- summer solstice in 1983, when Ben came to the Pagan Spirit Gathering, waiting for him at sunset/moonrise
- writing
- playing Mozart
- dancing in Solstice circle

- gliding/soaring
- nursing my children

I had learned and was learning
- that despite losses, I have survived. "I" am still here and have grown stronger.
- the futility/wrongness of trying to control anything or anybody
- to relax
- that there are endless chances to grow and endless forgiveness
- that in the end everything will be OK.

But Bolen also mentions humor, and introduces into the old story of Demeter and her grief for Persephone, the less-known figure of Baubo: the bawdy, post-menopausal woman who makes Demeter laugh. Angela, my friend, was often my Baubo, but now *I* had to *become* her—that aspect of the laughing crone who is also a child—she who both precedes and follows the maiden and mother in the cycle of rebirth. I noted that I had had a young girl—a child under seven with me for the previous seventeen years—Julie, then Rebecca, then Laney. Julie the child was gone. Laney's childhood was disappearing before my eyes. The child I myself had been disappeared in the years soon after my sister had died. How to recapture that child, to be her again, to bring her along? It came to me that as I had relinquished the child (as I did at puberty) and the maiden (as I did when I became a mother), at age 48, I had to relinquish the mother, or at least reclaim her in new ways.

I noted that it took the green candle a lot longer to burn out than I had anticipated: I thought it was all but gone and yet it flickered still, two hours after beginning. I thought of blowing it out like a birthday candle, but no, this was not to be decided by me. I was not on my own schedule.

147

I made a list of what I would still like to do in my life:

- to sail
- to look into becoming a mime
- to go deeper into writing
- to "finish" all the Mozart sonatas
- to be more open
- to take more risks of ego
- to find my sense of humor
- to find more time with Ben
- to stop smiling at everyone
- to learn more tai chi
- to learn more about gardening
- to explore

Before bed, I made a willow wand wreath, went walking and saw more deer. I also saw a wasp try to kill a monarch butterfly, but the monarch flew free. That night, I woke to strange shadows on the tent. I went out and saw the crone moon shining directly into the clearing—it was very bright, even though the waning moon was nearly half gone.

When I woke, the sun not yet over the eastern ridge, it was cold, about 50 degrees. I lit the white candle and thought of my talk with Selena: about being women at this time in our culture, of our aspirations and our relationships to our men, and of summer slipping by. She gave me a small plaster figure of a smiling witch, and we talked more about the version of the Goddess called Baubo. Feeling refreshed and renewed, I packed my things and left.

Decades later, the concept of "croning" or conducting rituals for making the passage to that middle stage of a woman's life have become quite common. There was even a "crone village" at the national Pagan Spirit Gathering I attended in 2011. However, the process had become, it seemed to me, too organized and too communal. Accepting the end of my periods and that stage of my life was an intensely personal quest, not one that I shared or wished to share with many others. And yet I acknowledge that there is a comfort in knowing that you are not alone in going through your changes. Still, I have found that only in solitude do I ever really get in touch with what I need to do next.

So both witches will remain on my book shelves for the present, reminding me that life—indeed, the universe—is not as scary when viewed through the androgynous crone's lenses of age and experience, *if* you are willing to pull her dress over your head.

Baubo Wanders

i. Setting Sail

Midsummer dawn, Baubo
crouches on shore
a long time
staring at the crooked
skeleton of her lists,
her calendars, her maps,
her guidebooks
that have fixed
where and when and who
she is.

Uncoupling bone from bone she
stacks in an inverted cone, and
touches flame. Bone-fire
blossoms into smoke.

Sparks swirl like veils
of confetti or rice.

She trembles to see
itineraries of her life
burn away.

There is only now.

She feeds the fire, first,
calendars locating her
on coils of time: celluloid frames
zipping through suns and moons,
reeling into the past,
filling in emptiness.

Next, maps of stars, of islands,
continents and waters, maps of
reefs, of her body,
charting mystery,
showing how to maneuver straight
from here to there.

Then, her endless lists
of things to do,
agenda brooking nothing
unforeseen, notches
on the belt of her life.

Baubo shreds them all,
tenders them
to sharks of flame.

Shedding tears,
tearing up her lists,
her maps, turning her back on calendars,
no longer believing in them,

letting schemes and plans
burst like bubbles of champagne
over the prow of her journeying,

she sifts colored sand
into a pattern, then
scatters it,

unsticks a little vessel
from sand and sets sail,
slipping canvas and rope
through the riggings,

loops of line holding sails
in place, tacking her
loosely to the present.

Without written guides, she attends
the enormous
freedom of the sea,
the intense listening,
the fierce intelligence just beneath.

She feels volcanoes and icebergs
burgeon below, thermals mushroom
soundlessly above.

She senses the smallness
of her craft
and the immensity of
what is silent.

Venturing, she turns
and turns, dancing
on the dizzying
deck, unwinding.

Once disoriented, she sets
in the bow a poem:
touchstone,
compass with no point:

May it be beautiful before me,
May it be beautiful behind me,
May it be beautiful below me,
May it be beautiful above me,
May it be beautiful all around me.

I am restored in beauty.

I am restored in beauty.
I am restored in beauty.
I am restored in beauty.
I am restored in beauty.*

Shirt and sails pocket
the change of winds,
select her direction,
begin to convey her
across the deep.

a traditional Navajo prayer

(For the rest of the poem, see Avatars of Baubo *(Green Fuse Poetic Arts, 2013. Note also the similarity to my adolescent "autobiography" described herein on pages three-four.)*

Twelve:

Pursued by What I'd Once Ignored

One key to a happy marriage, I've finally discovered, is maintaining an awareness of what matters most to the other person and doing whatever you can to help manifest it . One of the kindest gifts Ben ever gave me was the insistence that we spend money for a good piano. Doing so, he also contributed to the strength of our marriage, for this piano has fed who I am at my core. He has also given me diamond jewelry and, once, a designer nightgown from a small shop in Paris, but his encouragement that we buy the 100-year-old, re-built Mason & Hamlin piano meant so much to me, especially because it was his salary that allowed us to afford it.

Time alone in a marriage with children is a precious commodity, and one that constantly has to be negotiated. Ben and I traded off "personal time" in which we pursued our own singularities, just as we had to schedule time for just the two of us, apart from the whirlwinds of our children.

Sometimes I stole time for myself from the State of Wisconsin, where I taught basic writing classes for 26 years. Chained (unnecessarily, I believed) to my desk for forty hours a week, I learned to use some of those excess hours for writing poetry. Or I played hooky of a Wednesday afternoon, driving out to the "country" to spend some time hunkered down in the most hidden corner of nature I could find, whatever the season. Just sitting in a corner of a field of corn could return me to my zero coordinates.

The past piles up behind us: tattered junk trails from our ankles. As we age, one of our jobs is to sort through that pile and decide what we will keep, polish, renew, wear—pull up into present time—and what we will cut off—abandon to history. Life becomes a process of giving up what we thought we couldn't live without, of living only for the possibilities in the now, throwing the rest into the canyon. But sometimes things return "out of the blue": something we had left behind on the roadside, kicked out of the car, and which has followed us home at long last. Our scent lives in its nose. It belongs. It's hungry and demands to feed, to be fed.

Music was one of those abandoned creatures. One night I dreamed that I was being pursued by someone terribly disabled. I was terrified and ran, faster and faster, believing that I could outrun the deformed, limping person that was obviously struggling to overtake me. Finally, when I arrived at my apartment door, breathless and panting, I turned to find him already there, waiting for me. With sad eyes, he said, 'You don't even remember me, do you?' whereupon, pressing two tickets to the symphony into my hand, he turned and limped away.

The only use of my childhood spinet that had followed me faithfully from home to home for 15 years had been lessons for all three girls and for me to play and replay the few pieces that I had learned in my teens. And when I got bored with those, I "taught myself" new pieces. For instance I sight-read a Bach Toccata in D Minor but abandoned it when it sounded too much like the gloomy organ music I recalled from the Methodist church. I much preferred the one in G Major which the editor pronounced as 'insubstantial,' but which I loved for its brightness, joy, gaiety, and sheer brashness. Slowly I "worked through" all the Mozart sonatas and returned to scale and arpeggio work in order to strengthen my arms and fingers.

Still, it wasn't enough. One afternoon, waiting for one of my daughters to finish a music lesson at our local music conservatory, it dawned on me that I too could take lessons! My first husband, Luke, with whom I had remained in correspondence, urged me not to wait: he had returned to singing lessons in his fifties. So, with that encouragement I inquired, and soon, in my late fifties, took my first piano lesson in about forty years with Elaine B.. Our goals and tastes really matched, and she loaded me up with plenty of music to try: Bartok, Hindemith, Schoenberg, Prokofiev (my favorite). I also was given access to the conservatory's library of CDs. In addition, the lessons cost less than I had anticipated. I felt very lucky. I practiced (still do) about 45 minutes a day, but immediately noticed the difference between the pianos for use at the Conservatory and my 50-year-old spinet. Elaine told me that a serious musician needs a good instrument, which is what led to Ben buying me the Mason & Hamlin.

I checked out as many CDs of modern women pianists and composers as I could, including many played by Mitsuko Uchida, who soon became a favorite. I listened to more and more "modern" (i.e. 20th century) music, my ear slowly becoming more accustomed to its atonal qualities. I listened while I drove, especially on the jaunts with our dog, Maggie, into the country.

Of course, practice—pushing oneself—is the heart of any skill. In tai chi the hardest part was the standing work. Standing on one foot in the 'lift hands' pose for even a minute made my left leg cry out in protest at the burning. At home, practicing, I usually didn't push my limits or hold as long as we did in class. My thinking was that I didn't want to become a compulsive masochist about it, then wondered if it wasn't indeed necessary to 'suffer' (allow) some measure of discomfort to reach the level of strength needed. Mike, the tai chi teacher, as well as my current yoga teacher, Karen C. have pointed out that it's not the leg that freaks first; it's the mind. Relax the mind; strengthen the mind, and the leg will follow. The joy of creating the strength *to do it right* eventually overrides the discomfort (the *work*) of practice. Today I believe that finding the specific practice for which one has enough passion is the key. Any "practice" will do, but one must have the passion, the motivation, the love, or one won't keep doing it. For Ted Williams, it was baseball. For me, the piano was my first passion. My mother said that she never had to remind me to practice (though I always had to stop when my father came home from work).

In 1993 one of my inspirations came from watching a master practice tai chi in the park and wanting so badly to have access to that same effortless grace in my life, where it was most sorely missing. I wanted the strength to endure the tensions of life with my family without collapsing: the strength to resist the temptation to bring ambiguous and uncomfortable situations to an end by forcing things rather than allowing them to resolve in their own time. How could I practice this strength? What muscles could I call upon? What model could I soak in? I had no clear image of how to behave with grace with my own children. Society's idea is to take control—to force, if necessary. But true grace is a following of spirit, and to follow takes great strength. How would I develop it? Again and again, metaphorically, I hit the wrong notes, lost my balance, crashed through to a conclusion even though my execution had been lousy. How to remember, minute by minute, my true task? There was no "frame" around my practice time in life as there is around piano time or tai chi or yoga time. How did one carry what one learned there forward into the unconscious busy-ness of life? to keep the image of a grace full of strength before me as I interacted with my children, students, husband? to blend, merge, feel the weight of the other and yet not *be* the other?

My personal boundaries were, and still are, thin. Thus, I often over-stepped my boundaries to tell others "what to do": the couple I was counseling who wouldn't quit picking at each other; my class assistant with panic attacks; Ben's irritation at the need for house repairs; and so it went. Yet the reactions of these other people were not really my business. Some boundaries are necessary.

It was another man who spoke of developing the kind of strength I admired. Timothy Gallwey's *The Inner Game of Tennis* (1974) relied heavily on the Eastern notion of Zen. I read that the strength one cultivates is at first merely an awareness of error without judgment (for that too knocks us off balance). And then one continues to be open to the correction that will come. There is great strength in *not*-doing, *not*-speaking: to hold, draw out the holding in silence so that something beautiful and true may emerge. Obviously I was still turning to the *I Ching* as a teacher, and to Carol K. Anthony's *A Guide to the I Ching* for a female model of relationship.

* * *

Spring was late in 1998. In the middle of May, the lilacs were still tight little fisted buds. In June we spent a week in South Dakota with our children before summer school started—a far cry from the same trip Jamie and I had taken nearly two decades earlier. This time, instead of signs and omens, I thought simply about rock: the rock blasted and chiseled away by men to represent the faces of their heroes: Crazy Horse, Washington, Teddy Roosevelt, Jefferson, Lincoln. Of course, women also have egos, but somehow it seemed ludicrous to imagine women's faces up on Mt. Rushmore, having a cozy tête a tête—a 'good old girl' network. On the other hand, perhaps it's a good idea to keep our heroes'/heroines' faces before us—we all need models.

But perhaps we should not carve them in stone. No model is perfect, and reputations tarnish: e.g. today we know things about Jefferson and Roosevelt, for instance, that make them perhaps less appropriate as heroes than they seemed only a few years ago.

Though women's faces aren't carved into the Black Hills—or the list of famous twentieth-century composers, for that matter—the concepts of what constitutes a desirable woman and a good mother still seem to be pretty solid in our society. But maybe they are softening a bit as they prove too rigid, untenable. It still takes courage to let them crumble and fall down the mountainside, however, as one clings blindly to the side of the mountain, wondering who one is and which way one should go.

It occurred to me that it's hard to find the face already *in* the rock instead of imposing one's own. As I struggled to find my way to what's really right in my dealings with my children, husband, and my own instinctual self, I often felt like a pioneer, leaving the broad cultural highway of the accepted and forging my way—carving a new face on the very rock I was clinging to without surveying it first; without a model beforehand—only by listening within and to the one who speaks through the *I Ching*, dreams, silence, and art. The master sculptor leaves no trace. Models are not meant to be cast in stone, but to evolve, perhaps as a dance evolves in beauty and time, and clarity is made possible through the perseverance and experimentation allowed through discipline –then disappears.

Back home, I taught summer school and took the girls for horseback riding lessons during "free time." It was a rainy summer, yet there was more interaction with our immediate neighbors. The couple across the street, whose children were grown, separated for a while. The husband next door left his wife for another woman. Every day I had looked out my pantry window to see into their dining room where there were always fresh flowers in the middle of the dining room table, no matter the season. My assumption was that the husband had bought them for his wife every week. But they continued to bloom there even after he was gone. So it appeared that his wife was just another woman buying flowers for herself like the rest of us.

During that decade of our 50s, I was in a fairly negative mood about families in general—the conflicts therein, the lack of intimacy they provide, proportionate to the number of people in them. It seemed sometimes as if all five of us were in our separate bumper cars, ramming into each other as we went about trying to get what we each wanted. And we didn't apparently care about how hard we rammed each other, ending up stalled in a muddle, not going anywhere.

I read Barbara Kingsolver's new novel *Pigs in Heaven* (1993) about a woman in danger (she thinks) of losing her six-year-old adopted daughter. She runs away with her, only to find that, ready to give her up, she needn't. Her daughter is not lost to her. Losing a daughter is a primal fear, and not only for me, I think. Though I have seen, first-hand, what losing a daughter can do to a mother, and the guilt and anguish that it entails, I believe that these feelings are archetypal, as seen in the Demeter/Persephone myth, upon which Kingsolver's book is perhaps partly based.

Laney became obsessed with her baby book that summer, asking question after question about what being a baby was like—wanting to hear things over and over. Finally, as I wrote in the poem "Three Days at Lake Michigan, Summer, 1994," she asked, 'Momma, do you remember when I was a baby?' I answered 'Of course!' whereupon she said, 'Always remember it' and then turned away.

She was taking leave of her baby-hood, moving on, and she wanted to make sure it survived somehow, somewhere—in my memory, if not hers. It was as if my baby was telling me goodbye and not to forget her. It was sad because, for one thing, my memory is *not* so good, and many memories have already been lost. It was also sad because I was often just concerned with getting through my endless 'chores' and not really seeing the fleeting children/teens/young adults by my side. And finally it was sad because there would be no more children—no sweet, close, idyllic intimacy that only a baby can bring—ever again. Except maybe for grandchildren.

Despite all these family concerns, I knew that Ben had made it possible for me to have my time alone, to take up the discipline of playing the piano—for real—that I had abandoned decades ago. All the time, in our marriage, he had been watching and seeing what I really needed.

That was a kind of love I had never before seen or experienced.

directions for playing

life should be lived legato and
rock climbing sure as hell better
be legato for there is danger
leaving the ground on your own and
swimming is legato only because of
water which is very legato but not so much
as smooth crystal-linked ice or as staccato
as rain beginning to pelt your head
                                    learning anything
including how to be married is staccato at first though
the goal is legato but that takes practice which hopefully
will stitch together the staccatos and draw
them tight to the point where the strokes
are not even seen beneath the surface or
in the seam
                        there are those who stumble
up the stairs to enlightenment young and never
look down and those who take to water as babes and can't
remember when they knew anything but
legato
                    the woman in the lane next to me with her smooth
                        enjambment
between laps surely is one who started swimming when wet
behind the ears long after polio left its jagged blip on
the surface of some historical pool but for me learning
has been a life of sitting anxious on the edge and wanting it
enough to be willing to die if needs be while slapping
together staccatos hit or miss mostly not
getting it right rising and indeed plunging but not
in a good way though my crawl finally cobbled
together a compromise of air and water that
has got me eventually to the end
                                    and in the end
perhaps it's not anything we do ourselves to connect
just life sooner or later tired of expressing as separate

particles rising then falling back effortlessly into waves
like that magician's trick of stuffing scarf after scarf into a
fist then smiling and teasing out a billow of graceful knotted
    silk
or faceless paper-dolls with just the tiniest point of join

Thirteen:

"Like You, I'm a Bit Wordy, and Can Go on about the Most Trivial Thing Forever."

Despite returning to the piano in my late 50s, my sense of not having "done enough" with my life became urgent. What could I give that I already hadn't? what could I offer out of the deepest, most unique aspect of my being? and what is that? My own life experience which has led me to certain (and certainly) unique beliefs about things? My poetry? My journal writing? The bottom fear, echoing my mother's, was that the best of who I am would be misunderstood or judged unacceptable. So how does one learn 'to be of use,' as Marge Piercy says in her 1973 book of the same name? On some days I did feel "useful": talking with one of my children or with a student, who often said that our conversations were helpful. But beyond those small, seemingly inconsequential, external acts, I had to trust that internal acts are 'useful' too, and have consequence.

Once Richard Wilhelm (the Chinese scholar who first translated the *I Ching*) told Carl Jung this story:

> *In the ancient Chinese province of Kiaochou there was a drought so severe that many people and animals were dying. All the religious leaders attempted to solicit relief from their gods: the Catholics made processions, the Protestants said their prayers, and the Chinese fired guns to frighten away the demons of the drought. Finally, out of desperation, the town's people called upon the Rainmaker, and from a province far away there appeared a shriveled up old man. The old man immediately requested a small hut on the outskirts of town, where he locked himself up for three days and nights in solitude, and then, on the fourth day, it rained. In fact, it snowed at a time when snow was not expected.*
>
> *Wilhelm, who was allowed to interview the Rainmaker, asked him how he made the rain, and the old man responded by exclaiming that he did not make the rain, that he was not responsible! Not satisfied with this response, Wilhelm pressed on, "Then what did you do for these three days?" And the old man explained that he had come from another province where things were in order with nature, but here, in Kiaochou, things were out of order, and so he himself was also out of order. Thus, it took three days to regain Tao and then naturally, the rain came.*

I thought of this story of the Rainmaker—the one who helps balance the world by balancing him/herself. If I could really do that, it would probably have some effect. However, I was inconsistent, unreliable in my own balance, and our culture does not usually reinforce the value of such inner work, unless you are a cloistered nun.

Or there's Franny, in J.D. Salinger's *Franny and Zooey*, who tried, unsuccessfully, to "pray without ceasing" as we are told to do by St. Paul in the New Testament. Zooey is called in by their mother to talk with Franny as she falls into depression because of her inability to live up to that religious injunction: to pray unceasingly the "Jesus Prayer": "Lord Jesus Christ, have mercy on me." Her mother's chicken soup holds no comfort. What ultimately helps are her brother's words: "How in hell are you going to recognize a legitimate holy man when you see one if you don't even know a cup of consecrated chicken soup when it's right in front of your nose? Can you tell me that?"

One of my students, LaShawnda, came to our house one day to discuss one of her essays. In the essay she made the point that the character in the memoir we were reading weakened his argument by whining about how life had treated him unfairly. She then went on to contrast his life with her upbringing in the Milwaukee ghetto by drug-addicted, violent parents. She had *nothing* yet had overcome so much. And as she sat in my kitchen refusing my juice and muffins, I felt that she could have made a similar argument about me and my family. We forget, sometimes, how much we have.

I had several students like LaShawnda that summer, working hard, fiercely determined to succeed. I often wondered if I was 'doing enough'? too much? I prayed for them—LaShawnda, Sarah, Angelique, Chantell, Latasha, Val—but what 'good' could I do? Very little. Now I think perhaps I discounted—as many women do—what I might actually have been giving.

I remembered how my 'big sister' in my college sorority, upon my graduation, had inscribed a book to me which read, "I expect great things of you." In my mind, "great things" did not compute with making chicken soup or conferences with under-performing students. At the edge of my mind, always, was the need to make up for the lost opportunities of my sister and my mother.

I didn't feel as if I were contributing anything unique to anyone else's life. I felt quite replaceable. Starting to attend Quaker meetings, I often felt that I didn't do enough 'good works,' by which I meant saving, rescuing, chairing infinite committees, visiting the 'sick,' standing on inner-city corners in the rain where the latest drive-by shooting had occurred. I did not do these things. Though there were many who did these things—and more—out of noble motives, I mistrusted my own.

* * *

School started once more and my feelings of having accomplished so little were waiting for me, right in my office. I returned to a Jane Roberts' book, *The God of Jane*, in which "Seth," speaking directly to Jane's husband, said "that it was *not* our personal responsibility to change the world for the better. Yet, by following our own unique impulses, we impress our own vision upon the world naturally, which ultimately has a positive and creative effect." This was also what the *I Ching* was telling me, and I believed it to be true. I must be content, I thought, simply to be who and what I was in the time remaining—to be that completely and not to waste time and energy trying to 'accomplish' great works. I needed to have faith in what I was, in what I could yet become, in all the intertwined arenas of my life.

I had to laugh out loud at this line from one of my students' introductory essays: "Like you, I'm a bit wordy and I can go on about the most trivial thing forever." Leave it to students and children to nail your peccadillos. Yet through the commonplace, through 'trivia'—the three-way crossroads associated with the Crone—unexpected connections and possibilities arise out of the invisible world, which we would otherwise not see. When we put pen to paper or touch the keys of a computer, we are making invocation, risking being foolish or trite, trusting that, with perseverance, some new vision will break through the mundane.

167

Sounds good, but one of my students, Jason, who sat way in the back, made it clear that everything "sucks," daring me to "make it all interesting and relevant."

My supervisor at work encouraged me to apply for a system-wide teaching award of $5000. That was enough incentive for me to spend time creating and gathering all the documents necessary, one of which was my "Philosophy of Teaching." I found writing it an interesting process, once I started. Here it is:

My Philosophy of Teaching

    My philosophy of teaching is the flip side of my experience as a learner, and I still see myself foremost as a learner, taught by such things as mistakes, following rather than leading, and riding the tension between ideals and reality.

    I believe that any discipline/practice/craft will teach you what you need to know if you follow it with perseverance, over a long period of time. Writing can be such a discipline, though what you practice can be almost anything, as long as you love it (or sometimes love comes only after you have *to do it). But the practice can be anything you do a lot: over and over again. It could be the discipline of learning how to relate correctly to those we love; it could be the craft of music; it can be jogging or basketball or meditating or loving a child. It can be writing, which is what I have taught for nearly thirty years.*

    A craft is somewhat easier if you have a teacher who demands of you excellence—the very best you have to give. Sometimes if you don't have a teacher "out there," you learn to be even more honest with yourself, in terms of whether or not you've really done the best you can for the moment—whether your work/attempt has been slip-shod and habitual, or whether you have really been present, really there, to your practice and to your learning.

This does not mean that mistakes are disasters. Actually it is just the opposite. The greater the effort, the greater and more meaningful are our errors, and the more we can learn from them. I honor my own mistakes as indicators of what I need to learn, and I encourage my students to do the same in their essays (a word which means literally tries, attempts*).*

Writing is one of my own disciplines (to be disciplined means to be a disciple, a follower, a seeker of truth). I think that to be a disciple ultimately leads back to the truth of oneself. That is one thing that writing can do. Often I have discovered things about myself only by writing about them, being willing to follow words and images wherever they go, without having to impose my own agenda upon them ahead of time. This, of course, is the essence of creativity, along with its attendant risk, the letting-go of preconception. This willingness to be led "out" of current belief is, of course, the root meaning of e-duc-a-tion.

In the classroom, this "following" instead of "leading" gives each person the opportunity to reflect upon his or her current truth and encourages each person to contribute to the community of learning in his/her own way, honoring each other's truths, as well as the "new" truth that can emerge within the alchemy of community. This often involves more listening than speaking. Sometimes, being unused to silence, we can feel tense during these periods of quiet. But I think, again with perseverance, we can see the creativity possible through and within the tension of silence.

To me education is the process of drawing out the learner's truth—no matter what the "subject matter," *no matter what the craft or practice. Writing and reading have shown themselves to be, for me and for many others, processes that can teach people much about themselves.*

As a novice teacher, years ago, I would worry about "filling up the time," would concentrate on leading, staying in control, and was often the center of focus in the classroom. Over time, this has shifted. I have become more comfortable, as in my own poetry, with a structure that is more open-ended: that allows for more "following" of ideas as they evolve within a community of minds as we engage a text. At its best, this experience is like the exhilaration of riding a wave, knowing that you have developed the technical competency to do so. This creative experience within the discipline of craft is what I attempt to model for my students.

Over the years, I have also moved away from the physical classroom as the only arena for teaching. The partly online courses that I have taught for the past few years allow for a different kind of interaction than that of the classroom. Students often become more invested in their discussion comments when they must write them out for others to see. In addition, shy students are more likely to participate freely in online discussions, especially when they are well-structured. Nevertheless, I believe that there will always be a place for the classroom: the quick, often chaotic pace of direct, face-to-face interaction.

Incorporating the community through service-learning sections of "College Writing and Research" has also been a recent step toward widening the arena of learning for my students. Our college students are developing, not only their minds, but also their self-confidence, interpersonal skills, and ethical stances. Encouraging students to take the small risks of serving in a homeless shelter or literacy center in order to gather first-hand research has led to many positive results, as seen in some of my students' papers and online discussion forums. Students, separately and together, begin to question stereotypes, to accept ambiguity and the fact that there may not be quick and easy solutions to the large problems facing us as individuals and as a society.

Undergoing these processes, all aspects of their writing usually improve dramatically.

For all of my writing students, who are often quite unsure of themselves, I spend a great deal of time responding at length to their work—usually focusing first on what is working well, and building from there with lots of questions and "what if's." The criteria for good writing emerge spontaneously as students develop, through extensive revision, their core ideas, while giving and getting feedback from others. Revision then becomes a means of honoring their mistakes, which in fact, do teach them. Revision becomes a means of giving birth to creative thought, of making their ideas real, concrete, visible. The quotation over my computer, "The reason I write is to find out what I mean," is something that my students discover as they develop the craft of writing, whether it's expository or "creative."

I have tried to follow this philosophy in my own creative work, as well as in my teaching. Following my own interest in poetry and music, I have developed my own brand of hypermedia poetry, which I share with my students on my web page, and offer as an example of pursuing one's creative vision wherever it leads.

My mistakes, my craft, and my students have always led me to learn, are still leading me to discover how to become an even better teacher.

*   *   *

Despite the challenges of my late 50s, there were, as The Baker's wife sings in Stephen Sondheim's musical *Into the Woods*, "moments." I carved out time for my new piano and the new music I was discovering. The piano tuner recommended a $300 humidifier/dehumidifier system to help keep it in tune and to protect the refurbished soundboard. And it was thanks again to Ben, who gave up his fall clothing allowance, that we could afford it. Over and over again, he was there in the background, even if we didn't have time to talk very much, watching, seeing what was really important to me, and making sure that I had it.

My poetry, my piano are my "hands." If my relationship with my own parents severed them (as in the fairy tale), they grow back every time I have the space and freedom to create. That's why art is so important, and the opportunity to make it: it heals. But there are other opportunities to create too: through attitude, tolerance, belief, through what we envision, what we say.

One year, in mid-July, I had a week to work on my poetry alone at our new condo in Chicago while Ben stayed in Milwaukee with the girls where we still lived. Ben was moving up the administrative ladder and was now the provost of a large art school in Chicago. That summer I didn't have to teach (again, thanks to Ben's insistence), so for seven days, alone, I worked obsessively, compulsively, on a Flash hypertext poem "Bird Calls" about the death of my sister. Though the subject was sad, while writing about it, I was free. I had to remember to eat and get up for breaks. When I did, I walked to downtown Chicago to buy a printer and books of poetry (I wept over Mary Oliver's new book of poems *What Do We Know*), all of which I taxied back.

I tried not to think about what was going on back in Milwaukee. Guiltily, I felt the relief of being physically apart from them all for even a few days, just as I realized that I wanted to persevere: I wanted to try to set right the pain of the past, as well as, eventually, to give another recital, to put out a book of poems even if I had to do it myself, to get the medium-air sailing rating, and to keep going until I got the damn Flash thing mastered. I had to believe that I could and would do all the things that I wanted, even if I didn't yet know how, if I just went on trying to do them as best I could. If I just *practiced.*

After spending that time alone with the girls, Ben agreed to talk with my therapist, alone, about her work with me. A lot of that work had to do with learning how to find my voice in relationship with a man and to set boundaries in a family as large as ours. Both Ben and I felt the challenge of maintaining harmonious family relationships when during the week he was eighty miles away.

Ben said he had dreamed of the two of us in Paris. I was much younger than he and threatened to leave when an older couple wouldn't stop arguing. Laney dreamed that our family all took separate vacations. One of our great family challenges was to find ways of maintaining unity at the same time that life would, as we grew older, increasingly remind us of our separateness and individuality. Ben's individual passions were just as important as my own, and yet I didn't know what to do to further them. My salary at the time was merely 20% of his, so I could not insist that he do anything for himself with it, though I encouraged him to.

Perhaps Ellen was right when she said that I became involved in so many creative projects in order to escape the five-ring circus of our family. Perhaps she was partly right, but creating and learning—piano, poetry, yoga, swimming, diving, Italian—never felt like avoidances to me, though they were and still are sanctuaries, and perhaps antidotes to age. It is true that when I am not busy I become melancholy. Thinking of both my sister's unlived life, my mother's stunted one, and Jamie's and my broken marriage, I often dreamed of a house of unused, unlived-in rooms, which made me sad. However, if it's true that "nothing is ever over" and, as Lee Smith writes in her work *Oral History* (2011), "worlds continue to open up within the world we know," then perhaps all that's needed is openness to the possibilities in the present.

It seems to me that at any moment the story one has told oneself about one's life can shift, sometimes just slightly, sometimes profoundly. And I could tell stories about everyone whom I love, but they would be my stories, not theirs. We are connected, but perhaps one can never decipher another's meaning. Ben said recently that good fiction is a story centered on what someone wants. Perhaps that's true in a very basic way, but I think a person's story has more to do with

173

what s/he *creates*. Of course, creating is a desire, a passion, as well—perhaps the most basic one. But Ben and I were so involved with the girls on the weekends when he was home that we didn't have much time for each other. We seemed to share only about half of our lives, our "stories," but probably that's true of everyone at a certain stage of parenthood.

Practice at sailing, swimming, diving, working at the piano and at poetry brought me happiness—the freedom that comes through discipline to a structure—although it is a fairly solitary kind of happiness.

Yet my third marriage also brought me great happiness and deep satisfaction that comes from crafting a complex relationship over time. Richard Wilbur, in his poem to his wife, "For C," reads, in part:

> *there's a certain scope in that long love*
> *Which constant spirits are the keepers of,*
>
> *And which, though taken to be tame and staid,*
> *Is a wild* sostenuto *of the heart,*
> *A passion joined to courtesy and art*
> *Which has the quality of something made,*
> *Like a good fiddle, like the rose's scent,*
> *Like a rose window or the firmament.*

Children and pets bring a similar kind of satisfaction: that of learning, duty, responsibility, and shared *fun*.

On my fiftieth birthday, I took myself and my personal savings (with a little help from Ben) to Hawaii for a ten-day vacation. There, I had a wonderful time. I could go anywhere I wanted, when I wanted, without having to consult anyone else first. And yet—there was no one with whom to share the amazing sights, smells, and sensuousness that I experienced.

Happiness without the presence of beloved others, without the discipline of learning to live together, would soon wear thin, I believe, disabling the prospect of lasting joy. As Alexander McCall-Smith says in his novel *Friends, Lovers,*

Chocolate (2005), "Each of us is born into our own mysteries but the mystery of another might just take us in and embrace us. And then what a sense of homecoming, of belonging!" It is less a search than it is a jolt of recognition when one stumbles upon one's own brand of heart-soaring happiness. And in marriage, one has the additional responsibility to watch for, nurture what brings one's partner that same jolt, and hopefully be there to share in it.

* * *

In 2008 it turned out I needed a fifth breast biopsy but had to wait a week for it. I had had one benign biopsy in college, but as mammograms were said to be essential for women in their fifties, I dutifully had one a year, and for a span of about five years, had five "false positives" in a row. In 2017, the American Cancer Society (cancer.org) wrote this:

- *About half of the women getting annual mammograms over a 10-year period will have a false-positive finding.*
- *The odds of a false-positive finding are highest for the first mammogram. Women who have past mammograms available for comparison reduce their odds of a false-positive finding by about 50%.*
- *False-positive mammograms can cause anxiety. They can also lead to extra tests to be sure cancer isn't there, which cost time and money and maybe even physical discomfort.*

I have dense breasts, which further increases the chance of false positives. There was a new cluster of calcifications in my right breast, a bit more worrisome in shape than those a year and a half ago, but given my history still probably nothing. But the radiologist couldn't guarantee it to 98% and so it was up to me—biopsy now or wait six months. He was much nicer than the former radiologist (who had announced—before the biopsy results—that he thought I *did* have cancer but that he would "pray for me"), but I was still upset. In the meeting, to which Ben came, I found myself letting the two men take over the discussion of what was essentially a decision about my own body. Later, however, I relied heavily on Ben's comforting me with his belief that I would not die from breast cancer. I believed him, and, at least for the time being, it has been true.

Probably the early and sudden death of my sister taught me that I'd better develop alternate routes to happiness than family. The trick is living with the preciousness of particular people, allowing them their own idiosyncrasies, at the same time acknowledging the mortality of everyone you care about, including yourself, without steeling yourself against it. It wasn't and isn't easy. Perhaps I developed modes of happiness not dependent on particular others as a self-protective mechanism. Who knows?

* * *

The conservatory where I continue to take lessons offers scholarship auditions each April. These auditions serve several of my long-term musical goals: the money, of course, to keep taking lessons, but also to get over my fear of performance and of memorizing. My first audition in my first year of lessons went quite badly, but four things helped: Ben's steady presence and encouragement; my teacher's reminder that auditions are very different from performances and that flaws are inevitable; re-reading Hyde's *The Gift*, and vowing never to put myself through another audition (though of course I reneged on that). Terry Tempest Williams writes, in her 2012 book *When Women Were Birds*, "Perfection is a flaw disguised as control." At that time, it was still hard for me to accept the distance between what I could visualize and what I could actually create, but I think I'm getting (a little bit) better at it.

Ultimately, over the course of ten years, after I retired from full-time work in 2007, I gave five piano recitals (and am planning another), performing many compositions by contemporary American women composers, some of whom corresponded with me and generously sent me not only their scores but also their advice and encouragement. At the recitals, I asked my audience for, and received, donations to expand the conservatory's meager library holdings of compositions by contemporary women.

Today, I sometimes think of selling my piano as we consider "down-sizing" to a smaller home. I could always go back to playing on the pianos at the conservatory, I tell myself, though I would no longer have a piano here, at my fingertips. This year I asked my tuner what he thinks the Mason-Hamlin is worth today (I was told when we bought it that it was an "investment"). "Oh, about half what you paid for it," he answered. He said that sometimes, because fewer and fewer people buy pianos, they have to be destroyed and carted off to the dump. The thought fills me with horror. Many pianists or "keyboardists" today are choosing electric keyboards instead, many of which have become quite good as instruments. But I am not tempted.

There are places where the black paint on my piano bench and key cover is beginning to crackle and flake, but I religiously "water" the sounding board in the winter with the mechanism provided. I cannot imagine living without it now. Hopefully, someday, if the time comes, someone else will care for it, give it a home, use it as a strict but patient teacher, a means to *practice*: a safe—if temporary—harbor against the inevitable tempests in human relationships.

Fourteen:

The Gift of Thought

A poet colleague at work recommended Lewis Hyde's 1983 book *The Gift: Creativity and the Artist in the Modern World,* which immediately gave me a new perspective about my "art." In the introduction, he writes, "A disquieting sense of triviality, or worthlessness even, will nag the man or woman who labors in the service of a gift and whose products are not adequately described as commodities. Where we reckon our substance by our acquisitions, the gifts of the gifted man [sic] are powerless to make him [sic] substantial."

On one Sunday in August, someone in Quaker meeting said that she felt she didn't deserve God's love, mainly because of her many failures. She believed that she didn't deserve love because she hadn't achieved enough. Well, I couldn't let that pass. I piped right up, using a metaphor as usual. I spoke of photo negatives and the difficulty of seeing in them how things really are. But that holding them to the light—or better yet, developing them—was perhaps something we can do for each other. I often say things like that, but can't easily do them myself. I too become wrapped up in my frequent failures, my apparent lack of progress despite understanding what's required. Others might say that I am too hard on myself, but I am impelled by seeing something as indeed possible if I can just get out of my own way.

I should perhaps have listened to my own metaphor, archaic as it is—who remembers photographic negatives? or the need to "develop" pictures, which we now just snap and can instantly share with others through social media? Nevertheless, my remark in the Meeting was something crucial that I was myself in the process of learning. Perhaps we can't escape our dark view of ourselves except through the love of those who "hold us to the light." Ben and I were learning to do this for each other, though of course we had disagreements, often and predictably. I began to think of us as "push hands" partners—a form of tai chi in which one "feels" the movements of one's partner without forcing a response. Originally practiced as a form of military training similar to judo, "push hands" was a physical form of "not doing" in partnership which seemed alien and extremely difficult. But Ben was like a push-hands partner—there, but everything important was often unspoken. How different from my second marriage in which every aspect of our relationship was constantly analyzed and found wanting!

It helped to think of a lifetime as an unfolding rather than as a "progressing" toward something. On my way to the tai chi sword class one evening in May, I stopped and looked across the neighbor's back yard to a maple, already leafing out in those incredibly green blossoms, and on which I finally spotted the robin singing and singing. The willow leaves were also there, softening the yellow whips of the branches. There was still a little light, but not much. There was nearly a perfect balance, right there and then, of beauty, hope, and melancholy. And it struck me how old spring actually is: for how many millennia have robins sung, trees have leafed out perfect, glossy leaves, and rhizomes and bulbs have begun their old journey to that surface we call life. Another balance of opposites: the very old in the very, very new.

I reflected on Ben's occasional comment that I 'think too much.' Predictably, his comment started me thinking even more. The journal I have written most of my life has been my therapist, or, as my mother described hers, an 'escape hatch.' I realize that I've always been interested in autobiographies, letters, and journals, especially of artists. How have others thought about their lives and their art? how have they rafted through the whitewater of relationships and family? balanced creativity and spiritual seeking with the "quotidian" (to use lawyer/poet Wallace Stevens' term for the everyday)?

In October, 1942, when his daughter Holly was 18, Stevens wrote this to her: "That your parents—any one's parents—have their imperfections is nothing to brood on. They also have their perfections. Yr [sic] mother has them to an exquisite degree, tough as she is. The blow-ups that we have are nothing more than blow-ups of the nerves—when they are over they are over. [...] My own stubbornnesses [sic] and taciturn eras are straight out of Holland and I cannot change them any more than I can take off my skin. [...] We both love you and desire only to help you and part of yr [sic] education is to get on with us and part of ours to get on with you. Love, Dad"

I loved reading this, being reminded that the man whose careful, exquisite use of metaphor I wrote about in my dissertation could dash off such a letter about his "stubbornnesses" to his teenage daughter!

Admittedly, there is a difference between letters and journals. But I have found the journals of others—especially those not originally meant for publication—to be fascinating in that one can follow the process of another person's thought, and perhaps learn something from it.

I do not accept that I 'think too much." Howard Gardner's 1997 book, *Extraordinary Minds,* continues his earlier discussion of "multiple intelligences." He writes that reflection, the "regular, conscious consideration of the events of daily life, in the light of longer-term aspiration" has value. "We cannot assume that lessons from experience will automatically dawn on us. We are well-advised to devote effort to understanding what has happened to us and what it means." He goes on to say that the process of "*framing* is the capacity to construe experiences in a way that is positive, in a way that allows one to draw apt lessons and, thus freshly energized, to proceed with one's life.... *Critical* is the capacity to see not so much the bright side of a setback as the learning opportunity it offers—to be able to take what others might deem an experience to be forgotten as quickly as possible and instead to reflect on it, work it over, and discern which aspects might harbor hints about how to proceed differently in the future." I believe that my journals do this, but that too often I become bogged down in negativity. Yet I still believe that my journals, in which I write to discover what I think, hold the very best of what I am as a human being, even if they do not survive me.

Andy Goldsworthy's book *Time* (2000), on which the documentary of the same name was based, resonates strongly with this belief, especially that limitation is essential to the creative act, that destruction is part of the process, that beauty does not avoid danger or difficulty, but "walks on thin ice." Time, of course, the eponymous title of his book, is the greatest limitation of all. He writes, "I have tried to pitch my life so that I make the best use of my time and energy. Perfection in every work is not the aim. I prefer works that are fashioned by the compromises forced upon me by nature, whether it be an incoming tide, the end of a day, thawing snow, shriveling leaves, or the deadline of my own lifetime." Reading and seeing his work helps me to find more peace with the concepts of transience and loss, seeing them instead as continuity and flow.

I continued to see my psychiatrist and therapist. I had a dream in which my therapist's skull, with my lucky number

27 on it, illustrated how the bones of my mind were knitting together in new ways. That was helpful. My psychiatrist said I would "know" when I was ready to go off the anti-depressant, though he added that "my story would always be my story" and that a significant trauma before the age of ten will leave a long-lasting mark. But I've come to believe, reading other people's stories, that one can learn to create new, more interesting narratives. And that involves the gift of thought.

Unfortunately, as of today, according to the United Nations, two-thirds of the illiterate people in the world are women. Programs like *Women for Women International*, to which I give monthly, are attempting to change these statistics, particularly in countries ravaged by war. And in the United States, according to Wikipedia, "In 1967, women surpassed men in number of bachelor's degrees conferred in the United States, and more bachelor's degrees have been conferred on women each year since. Since 2005, the majority of degrees in each category (including master's, and doctoral) have been conferred on women in the U.S."

I was graduated from college in 1967, so it seems as if that was a turning point for women's education in the United States. In high school, I was encouraged to keep my thoughts and curiosity to myself, especially if it challenged conventional thinking. Hopefully girls will never again be encouraged (as I was) to hide their intelligence from a boy so that he would like them and not be intimidated by them.

Even though these last statistics are hopeful, I am ever aware that a high level of literacy—with the critical thinking, imagination, and aspirations it brings—are not within the reach of many girls AND boys, in America and around the world, who do not live in areas wealthy enough to support the teachers and schools necessary. And we all remember that it was not so long ago that a young Pakistani woman was shot because she advocated for the education for women.

This troubles me more than I can say. I think about it a lot.

Wild Rhubarb

—for Malala Yousafzai

Once upon a time
in the wilderness of puberty

a girl swore to strive
for perfection in all things.

She vowed to excise
the outlaw in herself, so

began to weed.
One day she knelt,

pulled off the toughest plant's
toxic leaves, then spied

the wrist-thick rhizome
burrowed in red, hard clay.

She began to dig,
and as she dug was learning something

about determination,
about the deep, wild beauty

of imperfection: that
one day girls like her,

who seem to submit, whose minds
are never allowed to gather light,

will run renegade,
and through the densest matter, despite

desecration by
the fiercest gods, thrust forth

from earth's succulent belly
lush throngs of thicker, greener,

even darker, shoots.

Fifteen:

"If You Have Creative Work, Nothing Else Matters"

Barbara Pym is, in my opinion, a vastly underrated English novelist of the mid-twentieth century. In her novel Jane and Prudence (1953), her character Jane makes the following comment:

Creative work, that was the thing, if you could do that nothing else mattered. She sharpened pencils and filled her fountain-pen, then opened the books, looking forward with pleasurable anticipation to reading her notes. But when she began to read she saw that the ink had faded to a dull brownish colour. How long was it since she had added anything to them? she wondered despondently....A line came into her head. Not one of all those ravenous hours, but thee devours....*If only she were one of these busy, useful women, who were always knitting or sewing.*

Then perhaps it wouldn't matter about the ravenous hours. She sat for a long time among the faded ink of her notebooks, brooding....

In my 50s, I was feeling that same kind of creative isolation until, one July evening near the turn of the millennium, some poetry friends invited me to join them in a backyard reading. It was wonderful, reading and listening to poetry being read by the light of a citronella candle. We tentatively agreed to meet often—the following week at my house. It felt wonderful to be connected again, particularly with good poets about my age. It had been one of my goals for a long time and appeared suddenly to have been met. One of the women poets gave me a book of poetry (*A Formal Feeling Comes*, 1994) written in various traditional poetic forms by women, one of whom was Maxine Kumin, who says this: "[It is] for me, the paradoxical freedom form bestows to say the hard truths. Constraints of rhyme and/or meter liberate the poet to confront difficult or painful or elegiac material, often elevating the language to heights unattainable in free verse, to say nothing of the extra music form admits." This led me to experiment with various "forms" in poetry though, keeping with my dislike for dogma and strict formats, I learned to adapt them to my own needs.

Soon I became closer to a few of the women poets that I'd met, along with one man. We began to meet regularly to share drafts of our poems and stories. It was a practice I'd been looking for, for a long time. We still meet, and the morning after, I am always ready and excited to revise. We try to meet every other week, which encourages me to set aside more weekday time for my own writing. Soon, I started to think about creating a chapbook of some of my best recent work. This group proved to be a turning point for me in my writing. As with the piano, I needed honest and fair feedback as well as deadlines in order to turn my writing into anything approaching a real discipline. Slowly, more of my poems were published, and I even won a few small prizes for poems here and there, and was asked to read at various venues. These things helped me to feel more on an even footing with my peers who wrote poetry.

I was also inspired by a 70-year-old poet who talked honestly about the challenges of being a poet, especially in these days, but who also encouraged me with talk of bravery and valor and the joy of process. Retired from a full-time job as a publisher, he wrote many years only over his lunch hour and an hour in the morning. And yet he achieved a lot. I thought of the saying I'd heard in different contexts, "Work sometimes comes from inspiration, but more often inspiration comes from work."

The poetry group helped to keep me focused on such work, resulting in a new chapbook manuscript called *Ties that Bind,* which I sent out to many possible publishers. I found that being on anti-anxiety medication, which my therapist convinced me to start in my early 60s, did make me more relaxed and positive about what I did produce. At least I attributed the change in my feelings to that. A third woman joined our group, and I continued to find the feedback I got there hugely supportive.

Some serious events involving the welfare of our children (which I have chosen not to discuss in detail here) called Ben and me to new levels of parenting as we approached the age of sixty: to stay calm, let go, and trust the process. It was difficult, but we both knew it was essential. In addition, I found myself feeling less invested and responsible for those of my students who really didn't seem to be making an effort. I still liked getting to know my students one-on-one through required conferences, however. It made them less scary to me, and me to them, I suppose! I was pleased that things seemed to be going better in the freshman seminar, though its emphasis on the transformation and pain of passing through to adulthood constantly reminded me of my daughters' troubles. In my dreams, my mother was becoming stronger— physically, mentally, emotionally, more confident. I started a poem in the pantoum form about such changes and, as Kumin said, learned even more discipline by experimenting with traditional forms.

Despite all this, I still felt the need to 'give' *more*, but still didn't understand what that meant, for me. Maybe it's a 'gift' to allow others to 'give': teaching service-learning at the freshman level, for instance. Maybe it's a 'gift' to be open to another's explaining something to me, even if I think I already know it. Maybe it's a 'gift' just to be open, without expectation. I remember Lewis Hyde's point that giving builds connections. Beneath and beyond all surface events still lurked basic questions about the connection of my identity to that of loss, which I needed to revisit, and did, through writing. I think again of Lee Smith's wonderful statement in her book *Oral History*: "Nothing is ever over, nothing is ever ended, and worlds open up within the world we know."

This led me to think about how routines can be comforting and expansive at the same time: how each instance of doing something "routine" overlaps or overrides or merges with, in some way, all other occurrences of the same experience. How the context for each is always a little different, like different washes over the "same" painting. On a different level, I think, perhaps each of our lives is a "wash" over the basic structure of life, enlarging and enriching it. And, of course, if we live many parallel lives, the same thing holds, but infinitely expanded.

The following poem of mine was inspired by one of Edward Hirsch's concerning the death of his son, 22, from a drug overdose. I recommend his *Gabriel: A Poem* to anyone who has ever suffered the loss of a child, or who has had to stand by helpless as a beloved child suffers. I wish my mother had been able to read it.

Palimpsest: Painting her again

*I keep scraping the canvas
And painting him over again
But he keeps slipping away* —Edward Hirsch (*Gabriel,* 2014)

Putting her fragments
Together in yet
Another way

Turning her differently-aged
Profiles this way and that
So as to see new things

In different lights
Even though the outcome
Is always the same

Putting her repeated death
Against once-future events
Casting it into differing perspectives

The cherished daughters
Arriving years after
The fact of loss

Connecting her to a whole
World of living relations
Memories

Shaded with deepening insight
Never-before-seen colors added
To my basic box of crayons

Foreshortening my grief
Triangulating its source
As I scribble wax over oil

Still trying to get
A fix
On sorrow

Sixteen:

"A Woman Who Lives Long Enough May Finally Be Told She Has Done Worthwhile Work"

A character in Marilyn French's novel *In the Name of Friendship* (2008) says, "A woman who lives long enough may finally be told she has done worthwhile work." When I was sixty, I won a state-wide prize for one of my poems, which I was asked to read at a bookstore in Madison. I read three poems and felt encouraged by the response. People came up after to tell me (separately) something positive about each of the poems I'd read. It felt really good. I felt at last as though I had finally given something valuable, something "of use." With some of my prize money I bought new books of poetry: Sharon Olds'

Selected Poems, Jorie Graham's *Overlord* and *The Dream of the Unified Field,* Louise Glück's *The Wild Iris,* and CK Williams' *The Singing.* It felt like ploughing seed back into my own work.

It was also satisfying that three of my composition students won prizes in the freshman writing contests that year. It would have been better if so many—most of whom were black—had not dropped out before the semester was over. Two of the three winners were white. But not the third, whose essay was about her service-learning experience at the Rescue Mission, which had helped her to come to terms with memories of her own childhood homelessness. And she remained in college.

Thinking more about the quotation from French's character, "A Woman Who Lives Long Enough May Finally Be Told She Has Done Worthwhile Work," I wondered: how long is long enough? who actually tells her—the world? her peers? herself? the dead? and what counts as "worthwhile work"— worthwhile to whom? for what?

As I look at the figure immediately to the left—the woman carrying a load of water—I think of several things. Carrying water, gathering food, preparing meals, of course, are all the work of survival—so important (worthwhile) and taken for granted that those who do them (historically, women) are rarely acknowledged or even paid. And if they are paid, the latest figures from Wikipedia indicate that women still earn only 79-82% of what a man earns for the same work.

I was lucky to have received modest acknowledgement for my creative work. But what if a woman is carrying a load of unpublished poems or novels or unperformed symphonies on her back? a lifetime of inner work? Such work is rarely acknowledged as important or even worthwhile (see again

192

Lewis Hyde's *The Gift*). If she is of a certain mind, and, again, lucky, she may acknowledge the importance of the work to herself. It may be important to her to work through grief, for instance: it may also be important to the past and perhaps future generations that this work be cleared. Obviously, because of my sister's death, I have thought about these things a lot. Here is an example:

Survivor: Banking on It

> After many lives, maybe something changes.—Louise Glück

i.
She was my babysitter, bodyguard,
my buffer between me and our parents. In return
I brought her napkins of crumbled cake from birthday
parties, crayoned for her the letters of my name.

Had I not been held down
in 1952 and pumped full
of gamma globulin I should have died,
would have caught the polio that killed my sister.

Before, I didn't really know
that anyone could die; after, my body
quickly learned: stomach cramped and skin
peeled; to swallow and to sleep were perilous.

Hunched over my journal, I kept secret
what metaphors came to me as cure.
Re-caulking with words what had been nearly swamped,
poetry's rites ferried me from death.

Pedaling furiously toward the piano teacher's
house, practicing daily until they pried
me away, playing for time, my greed
for music's waves carried me toward life.

ii.

Here's a hard one: what happens, in the
end, to the art a survivor
creates? Is it carefully gathered in and
counted to pay life's debt to the dead

for years cut short? the dead who spend,
alone, what passes for time? Has it
been enough to justify my
survival so far? How much farther?

Or is it just as carefully hoarded, talents
allotted to my next life, not
to have to begin again at zero, notes and
lines gifted to new fingers, new

voice, bearing compound interest?
I envy those free to improvise,
for the fun of it, a riff, a life, simple interest
coined and plunked freely into the collective.

But for me, creating is serious business.
Her sweet, empty mouth still hungers for my
crumbs. If I save anything for myself,
it's to an unnumbered, sequestered account.

No one must ever know if, when, or
what I cash in.
No one must ever glimpse the furtive, unearned
joy I take.

Yes: I did take joy in my creative work, no matter the outcome. My spring scholarship audition did not go really well, but I soon recovered and chose new music for the following year. The judge's comments about coloring and dynamics brought up issues with my performance that I could actually do something about. I could *improve*. I did plan a recital of contemporary women's compositions, perhaps for spring of 2006. My young male teacher said sardonically that maybe we could "sell t-shirts."

* * *

That summer, Ben was gone for two weeks to London on business, and I found myself, as usual, missing him. At the same time I felt guilty about my freedom to do pretty much as I pleased over the summer while he had such a heavy work load—work that *no one* would doubt as being "worthwhile."

I found myself reacting to Alix Kate Shulman's memoir *Drinking the Rain* (2004) in which she described living for several months, at age 50, on an island off the coast of Maine with no electricity or running water. She writes, "My new rules are few and simple: follow my interest; go as deep as I can; change the rules whenever I like." She was coming off years of work, parenting, lists and deadlines. Her children were grown and she was estranged from her husband. She came to write but found it hard to give up schedules and the idea of achievement. Her epigraph is from Kafka: "You do not need to leave your room. Remain sitting at your table and listen. Do not even listen, simply wait. Do not even wait, be quite still and solitary. The world will freely offer itself to you to be unmasked, it has no choice, it will roll in ecstasy at your feet." She finds this to be true: "the more lavishly I spend time, the more I seem to have, like the wild leaves I pluck for salad which grow more lushly, the more I pick...."

Her discoveries reminded me a bit of Thoreau's Walden experiment, but then I remembered reading that he did not do his own laundry; instead, he walked back into Concord once a week to have his mother do the (unpaid) work of washing his clothes.

Shulman, who, I am sure, found a way to do her own laundry even without running water on that island, went on to write, "After half a lifetime of adapting to the needs of others in the high tide of family, with no one to ask or answer to, I'm beginning to see who I am when the tide goes out." I found myself envying her—a little—for I was sixty years old, and still constantly having to "adapt to the needs of others."

While Ben was gone I tried different methods of managing my anxiety about our children's problems. As they grew into adulthood, their issues increased: relationships, finding and keeping satisfying paid work, and doing the difficult inner work required by illness. Bringing a child safely through to adulthood is a "weaning" process for the parent as well, and much of that involves letting go and setting boundaries. However, for me, these were always charged tasks (as I believe they are for many mothers) because a part of me did NOT want to "let go." Much of my self-esteem came from any evidence that I was a "good mother" in that (unlike my *own* mother) I could supply whatever they needed. (If I had been Thoreau's mother, I'm sure I too would have washed his clothes. And, worrying about his keeping warm in that shack of his in the Massachusetts winter, I would probably have added a couple of quilts!) As our daughters grew to adulthood, though, the idea that I could supply whatever they needed became patently false. Once again, like my own mother, I was face-to-face with my own Powerlessness—the Powerlessness to make things "OK" for those in my family. They had their own "work" to do and ultimately had to do it by themselves. Julie and Ned (her fiancé) both graduated from their respective programs in May, and we celebrated as we looked forward to their wedding in 2006. Julie talked about having children soon. And so the process would start again, for them.

Throughout my life, I have found it generally to be true that when I am alone, with no external responsibilities, my anxiety falls away. However, such times alone have been rare. They are almost impossible if one has both children and a demanding job outside the house. I tried, that summer when I didn't have to teach, to resist the calendar and clock that constantly reminded me of how little "free" time I had left. Yet, without a schedule, there was the temptation just to sleep (for I was always tired), or to let myself be completely taken over by household and family concerns: call the electrician, get the car's oil changed, worry about all my children's problems.

But Shulman writes that, eventually, "the anxiety I suffered only months ago, over the state of the world and the weight of my years have fallen away, replaced in this tranquil space by acceptance of what I find, of who I am. *Amor fate* goes the Latin proverb now tacked up over my desk: accept what is—literally, love fate."

The kind of solitude Shulman describes has always seemed the ultimate luxury, and yet I wondered if there was not a part of me that resisted it—fear that I would come smack up against my limitations. Though I was happy to plan a piano recital for next year, to work on my heavy-air sailing rating, and to send out more manuscripts, these were all achievement-driven and were only partly PLAY—the timeless attention that Shulman speaks of. It felt as if I didn't have TIME to PLAY, or if I did, that little "worthwhile" would surface. I did believe what Kafka said about the world rolling "in ecstasy at your feet" if you just give it your total attention, but I had rarely experienced it, and a part of me did fear it.

I took pleasure in continuing to meet the occasional needs of my grown children. Rebecca would call to ask me to read her (eventually published) manuscript or to ask me how to boil rice; Julie would call to ask how to get a wasp out of her house or to seek consolation for the huge bite taxes took out of her new income as a public health nurse. I loved that they *did* call, and I felt good that I could help in these small ways, even if it just meant listening.

*   *   *

That summer I was told that I had "galloping" cataracts that must be dealt with quickly. My mother had also developed cataracts in her 60s, but at that time there was no surgery for that condition except removal of the clouded lenses, after which she had to wear very thick glasses.

However, today there exist replacement lenses that can be inserted right into the eye. Nevertheless, I worried that, because of my fragile retinas, which had previous tears, I might lose my vision, which played a big part in most of the work I did.

While waiting for my surgery, I took advantage of opportunities to sail with new woman friends. I became more confident of my skills, though I sprained a wrist in the process. Eventually, by taking a class, I received the long-anticipated "heavy air rating," meaning that I could sail in winds above 12 knots (almost 14 mph).

The impending operation on my eyes produced another poem about the "worth" of one's own "vision" and its questionable use to others:

Depth Perception

Perhaps deep in one eye's concavity
the film of retina starts to peel from the globe

loosing scads of floating cells, flying
flocks of dark fish schooling from one

side of flicked attention to the other;
or the translucent sliver of lens,

meniscus, thickens from crescent to full and a fine
white nimbus washes over everything

like imagined sun at noon in Thebes.
But the remaining shutter blinks, and shots

are taken, processed, developed in the chemical
wash, the dark moonless inscape of the brain.

Two-dimensional negatives are stored
against the loss of fading three-dimensioned

positives, against the possible loss of
either limb of sight, those matched

nubs, until now drinking in,
organizing space and light.
                              How little

we deserve the good or bad that over-
takes us: Tiresias changed to a woman

for striking copulating serpents with
his staff, and seven years after,

transgendered once more for striking
them again. Then for telling gods

his blended view, the secret of woman's greater
ecstasy, Hera obliterated

both his eyes. A consolation prize
came from Zeus: second sight, a third

eye of little use to anyone.
How useful are gifts of ecstasy

or insight, in the end? Who listens
to translations of another's vision?

Eventually what's left is
a singularity of view, an old box

camera duct-taped together, one
widowed eye fixing one precious

part of one present in place, a spectacle
no longer casually paired, like sun

199

with moon, to plunge in tandem deep into the
delight of space, the seat-grabbing, doubled,

rounded ride, dancing eyes perfectly
fitted, synchronized, together shifting

easily from here to infinity, then back.

*   *   *

More poetry manuscript rejections came in, leaving me to ponder Shulman's quotation of Piotr Ouspenskii, a Russian mathematician and esoteric, who said that we all need the time to think "long thoughts." I needed to think about why rejection bothered me so much and why I wouldn't simply self-publish. I continued to go to concerts, when available, because they showed me what was possible (at least for men). I attended a day concert at the Milwaukee Symphony featuring Samuel Barber and Aaron Copland, and was comforted by the program notes for Beethoven's famous Fifth Symphony: how he often began with a mundane theme and then, instead of "building it up," "broke it apart"—deconstructed it—into greater and greater complexity, which was an image I really liked and hoped to emulate.

Thinking back to the statement that "A Woman Who Lives Long Enough May Finally Be Told She Has Done Worthwhile Work," I try, like Beethoven, to break it apart. Again I ask: how long is "long enough"? how old must we be before our work is recognized (if ever)? who would be doing the "telling"? and what defines "worthwhile work"? It's a simple enough statement, but contains all sorts of minefields if you are someone prone to self-doubt or to doubt about the quality or importance of your work. Why do we need outside reinforcement of our worth? Do women need this more than men? If so, why? Why doesn't our worth and the value of our work—whatever it is—go without saying?

200

I was indeed thinking "long thoughts" while alone, but they did not really comfort or enlighten me.

Ben arrived home, only to leave again the next day. We had only a few moments alone, but during those, he whispered to me, "I am never very far away," which immediately brought me to tears...

. ...and also inspired another poem that addresses the necessity of taking up the work of grief—that of the past, that of the present, and yes, that of the future.

Loss is ever-present, ever demanding our attention. Crafting it, exploring it, seems to me to be worthwhile work.

when you leave me

when you leave me
to go down under

anesthesia or high
above clouds to

another country skipping
a day or living it over

when you return
there is an understanding

we may be parted for good
there are places each

of us goes where
the other can't follow

through the caves of our separate
pain for instance calling

each other's name through
the crawl holes only

one can pass at a time
confusing my echo for your

voice one day
one of us will not

find our way back we say
we are ready we

have plans but there is something
stronger than even us

we will have to go
when it calls

Seventeen:

Piecing Together Beautiful Patterns from What Has Been Cast Aside

One day about ten years ago, going through my mother's "hope chest" (a cedar chest once used to hold a single woman's trousseau), I saw a quilt top that had probably been there for forty or more years. The pattern was an interesting design of blacks, blues, and browns. I hoped someday to get it backed and quilted. "About time," my mother would have said.

Julie and Ned (her husband) announced at Thanksgiving that they were expecting their second child sometime in early August, 2010, around what would have been my mother's 100th birthday. This was significant for Julie because she said it was my mother's example of the damage guilt could do that pushed her to "forgive" herself for Noah's prematurity in

2007, which in turn enabled her to take the risk of getting pregnant again. I had the quilt-top from the cedar chest finished as a Christmas gift for her, along with a happy picture of my mother and Marilyn as a baby.

Ellen, a fabric artist, knew of a way to put the photo and some text on the back of the quilt:

Quilt top by Clara (b. Aug. 1910)

Finished by Kathleen (b. March 1945)

Given to Julie (b. Aug. 1977) in December, 2009

Love, Wisdom, Forgiveness

Through doing this, I also seemed to be arriving on better terms with my mother and clearer terms with my sister even though no new memories of her had surfaced. Along with the picture I found of my mother was one of Marilyn and me. I was about six months old and she was ten years. On what would have been her 74th birthday, I lit a candle, thanked her for taking care of me and teaching me how to have fun, honored her courage and

independence and said goodbye, something I had never done before. Every day lived alters the past, no matter how slightly.

My mother, like other women of her generation, made quilts from scraps of old family clothes that had been outgrown or were otherwise unwearable. The designs of individual quilts were distinctive and creative. The quilt-top that I had finished for Julia was made primarily of wool pieces cut from what had probably been men's suits.

But there were other quilts that I had inherited, including one made specifically for me on the occasion of my first marriage. The pattern was one of a number of separate rings,

non-interlocking ones. I believe the name of the pattern is "Single Girl"—a fitting and predictive pattern, now that I think of it— as opposed to the more traditional "Marriage Quilt" of inter-locking rings. In the quilt she made for me, each ring is made of fragments of the dresses worn by my mother, my sister, and me from about 1930-1960, at which time store-bought clothes started to replace the ones made by women and girls. Like most women of her age and class, part of my mother's expected work was to make all of her and my clothes from patterns and material bought at "dry goods" stores. She made all of my clothes up to about 1960 when, at age 15, I was forced to make a brief, unhappy stab at learning how to sew. I learned the basics through a "Singer Sewing Course" for teenage girls, but my disregard for precision and my impatience for results made me a poor seamstress. Luckily for me, there were more and more affordable ready-to-wear dresses available soon after that, so I never actually made many dresses for myself (and never pants). Nevertheless, today, I recognize in the quilt my mother made and gave to me remnants of some of my favorite cotton childhood dresses. Like the oldest daughter in Alice Walker's wonderful story, "Everyday Use," in 1968 I did not appreciate my mother's gift for what it was, yet nevertheless displayed it on the wall of my first married home like an artifact from the past, which it was, but it was far more than that. Now when I wrap myself up in her creation at night, I feel the comfort of some renewed, if separate, connections to my mother as well as to my sister.

*   *   *

Clara, my mother, who was born into a poor rural family in 1910, had told me several sad stories from her childhood. First, she had never learned to ride a bicycle because her parents rebuked her for trying to learn on her older brother's bike. Nice girls didn't ride boys' bicycles. Second, she once tried to gather some green weeds for the chickens after one of her older seven siblings told her to. She worked hard gathering them and then happily threw them in to the chicken yard. But the chickens wouldn't bite. Her mother later told her they didn't like ragweed and that her brother had fooled her. Third,

Clara gave her doll the most beautiful name she could think of—Lucille. But her brother (no doubt the same one who told her to feed ragweed to the chickens) teased her and called her doll "La-Squeal." After that, she said, all pleasure in her doll faded.

It is clear that most of what my mother remembered as the youngest of eight was limitation, failure, and humiliation. As told and re-told to me, each such incident—and there were many—invoked so much great pain and hurt that they still seemed like fresh wounds. No doubt a "Highly Sensitive Person" herself, my mother was hurt by Everything. Her hair turned gray at age sixteen, and she always felt self-conscious about looking older than she was. Sometimes people mistook her for my grandmother. Her mother continually compared her to her older, more self-assured sister. Uncertain of her own coping abilities, she came to bruise under the lightest touch. It was as if those chickens were guilty of hurting her because they wouldn't eat what wouldn't nourish them, even if it was offered with love. Perhaps because her family had teased and criticized her so much, she turned to the promises of the Methodist Church for solace.

For much of my childhood and early adult life, in her presence I felt like one of those chickens. If I rejected misinformed ignorance, bad diet, the dogma of Methodism, television—anything my mother was, had done, had made, or believed in—I 'hurt' her, and the bruise bloomed right then before my eyes. I wondered at times if I would ever be free of causing her hurt, pain, and fear. Combined with my father's over-solicitous, protective domination, my mother's life seemed to me like that of a prisoner. My very being—who I was—seemed to hurt both of them. Even when I was almost 35, my parents saw only the tip of me. I had never been the "good girl" that my sister was. I was not obedient and compliant. When my mother had had asthma attacks, a defiant three-year-old me had stood on rocking chairs and had done every other thing I was not allowed to do while looking her straight in the eye. I challenged my mother's religious beliefs and my father's racism. I wanted to go to college far away, and did, even though my father said he could afford it only because my sister had died, a tactless and unnecessary remark which made it seem to me like "blood money." Until I did leave for college "back East" in Ohio, living with my parents literally made me sick with constant and mysterious stomach, skin, and respiratory issues, the latter no doubt influenced by my father's three-pack a day habit (he had started smoking cigarettes and cigars when he was twelve but quit in his 50s when our doctor told him what would happen if he didn't). A reformed smoker, he predictably forbade me to smoke if I wanted him to pay my college tuition, a challenge I equally predictably and immediately took up but nevertheless hid for the ten years I did smoke.

The oldest of three farm boys and the apple of his mother's eye, my father, Leonard, was definitely used to taking charge of situations. When my mother underwent surgery for fibroids in her late thirties, it was he and the surgeon who decided to removed her entire womb while she was under anesthesia, perhaps thinking that hysterectomy would cure her "hysteria" (anxiety). Had she wanted more children? Yes. Did they give her a voice in the matter? No. Did their decision hurt her? Of course. Was such a thing typical of most marriages of their generation? Probably. Since men typically brought all or most of the money into a marriage, decision-making was by default theirs unless they had an unusually outspoken wife, or one who also worked (and made as much money). My father was hard of hearing in a particular way: he could not hear the voices of women. He would understand none of this.

Did I underestimate my parents? Probably. As their child, I was certainly difficult. Desperately wanting to be "seen," I nevertheless hid who I was because revealing those feelings and thoughts appeared to be so threatening to them. I had not yet developed any skill in mediation or calm discussion beyond that of the classroom. I did not expect to be heard, seen, or understood, yet I carried my enormous need for all of these skills, not into the Church like my mother, but into all my relationships. I wondered whether it was ever OK for me to be "happy" when my mother was so miserable and my sister was dead. Eventually, I likened that question to whether it's OK to enjoy food in the face of world hunger. Unsteadily, I came to believe that when one cannot receive or share nourishment with another, it's probably OK to nourish oneself anyway.

As I became older, I gradually gained a better understanding of and compassion for my mother's pain and her life-long depression, starting in her childhood as the youngest, sensitive child of eight; continuing on as a girl fresh out of high school who was supposed to take care of her ailing, widowed mother, but who instead eloped with my father only to see her mother die the following year; and as a mother who found it difficult to conceive, losing her first child to the savage disease of pulmonary polio before she reached adulthood. Believe me, I got it, especially after I became a mother myself.

At times I could see flashes of the funny, irreverent woman she might have become, but it was always a ghost of something that had never fully materialized. And so I fought the things in myself that I saw had eaten her: anger, hurt, sadness, guilt, self-pity, isolation, envy, lack of self-confidence and self-worth. In my twenties and early thirties, there was a similar part of myself also convinced that the fact that I had no love and no rewarding job indicated that I didn't deserve them. Illogical, but it's how I sometimes felt. And that feeling reminded me of my mother, who of course never had the benefit of therapy for her life-long anxiety and depression. Instead, she took to the only art she knew, though she never called it that: the making of soft, warm quilts, of piecing together beautiful patterns out of what we had already outworn, deemed useless, and cast aside.

The quilt-top, now finished, still resides on Julie's present-day bed. She says that it comforts her, proof that my mother's quilting work was—as reflected upon in the previous chapter—both necessary and worthwhile.

Patchwork

Scraps like quilt patches
piece into patterns—

Wedding Ring, Crazy,
Grandma's Fan, Memory Charm—

bits unused, outgrown, unfinished,
basted together with tiny stitches,

themselves part of the plan,
part of the motif, seen anew

like the delphinium called
"larkspur" by my mother,

delicate, hard to grow from seed,
its blossom-laden spikes so heavy

they bend or break before blooming
unless staked stiffly with twine,

even in death magnificent, its many
waves of deep-sea blue folding in, reflecting

a grey change of weather and then
at collapse, the trio of dolphins

for which it is named, suddenly revealed, leaping
from the spent nectary of its very center,

but only at the very end of its life,
each patch is seen as for the first time,

set into a new design, like the blossoms of
elms she said she'd never noticed 'til she accepted

that blossoms could be green, could see
the bristle stuck in the oiled skin of the painting

the accidental tick of bow against the cello's mahogany back
the hard thump of ballerinas' feet that

call back the illusion created by frame and stage,
could see that transcendence is made of nothing

but the hair and wood and bone that limit it and yet
a poem must pass, like a quilt—

Bear's Paw, Ocean Waves,
Red Brick Road, Pinwheel—

through the coarse fine needle of the poet
like seed through shit, though she

hated that word, through
the lumpy messy chalice of earth,

no scrap thrown away, each
waiting in the sack to be selected,

reseeded, revised for possibility, how small
glances, she said, can fill the file of a whole life,

the way snow lies along a branch,
the sturdy curve of a neck

as someone stares out a window,
the sound of a bird whose name

she never knew, the belief
that she will never understand,

puzzles someone has to show her
how to solve, how time

curves space, what happens
if you move forward faster

than you fall, filling the quilt with variations
upon variations she finds lying

under her fingers; how the frame swells
with the texture of her thoughts, how

the universe expands, creating out
of nothing new space between galaxies

ex nihilo   ex nihilo   ex nihilo her
fool calls, smiling just

out of sight, how years go by and
her hands still weave in the same

lucky mistakes, manifest the same
peculiar elegance of imperfection, which,

when hemmed by community, quilted,
softened by some magic of connection,

tag ends of gossip and new
combinations of stories, forms

the passagework for draping wedding beds,
childbeds, everyday beds—

Plain and Simple, Spinning Spools,
Sunny Days, Love's Delight.

Eighteen:

In Which She Remembers What Has Not Yet Been Created

In 2011 Ben took a forced retirement and turned to part-time consulting work. I, on the other hand, after retiring from UW-Milwaukee in 2007, taught several *ad hoc* composition classes a year for returning students at Marquette University, my old nemesis.

I shocked myself one day in late September by walking out on my young, male piano teacher because of his discouragement and negativity. It was the last straw. He had said that I "always" chose pieces too hard for me and that I "always" took "forever" to work through a piece. He truculently agreed to "let" me play "Passages" by Rami Levin for him, though he said it "wasn't important" music. When I indignantly asked him what he meant by that, he said, "It isn't

Beethoven." Then, after I had played it through, he said that I had gotten it "all wrong." I stuttered around trying to defend myself—as well as Rami Levin—but then ended up leaving in tears and demanding another teacher at the front desk. The following week I started with a new piano teacher, a woman. Stefanie J. was then and is now supportive as well as demanding. I have never left her lessons "feeling like shit," as another of Aaron's former female students sympathetically commented.

Reflecting back on what Aaron had said that week, I did come to the realization that I had often made choices of difficult things—not because they are difficult *per se* but because they engage me in ways that safer, more predictable things and people do not. And in general I believe I have learned to live with the consequences, except for people who constantly remind me of how far I fall from their standards (as well as my own). I crave things that challenge and interest me, even if I don't do them very well. I suppose that also goes for my relationships. I used to fear mediocrity more than anything, but gradually, though my efforts in all my endeavors can be judged as less than stellar, the word "mediocre" didn't seem to apply as it might have, had I been simply satisfied to stay at the same level. But I had learned, and continued to make slow progress in all the areas that consumed me, and that was really all that ultimately mattered. The etymology of the word "amateur" is *amare: to love.*

A new online journal took three of my poems and invited me to enter their book contest next year. Steady progress. Diving and swimming were coming along well, thanks to a high-school lifeguard, Kaysha. She said that it had taken her a long time to learn the things I'd learned pretty quickly. I felt more and more comfortable on the diving board, jumping a little higher each time. We also worked on flip turns, made easier by speed and by tucking arms and legs.

Our girls were still going through the difficult challenges of early adulthood. I thought back to the rough times I'd gone through in my early twenties: married, teaching, back pain, no friends, and in my early thirties: marital problems, lack of job and single parenting. At those times there had been no medication and no sister or mother to talk it through with. I'm not sure that suffering through all that alone made me stronger or weaker. But it did make me realize that people will get through their own suffering (or not), and while a parent can listen and support, advice is probably no more helpful than it ever has been. Rebecca cheered me up one afternoon when, during a routine phone call, she said that she saw some connection between the "music" in my poetry and in her own writing. She also said (having returned to graduate school) that doing schoolwork was like kissing: you never really forget how. I loved the simile, which I never would have thought of myself, and stole it for a poem called "The Sensual Thesis" which was eventually published by the Wisconsin Academy along with another poem that won a prize.

I continued to think a lot about my sister's suffering and early death, but a dream showed me that her "crypt" was undergoing excavation and that there were peonies growing out of holes in the crypt. I wanted to ask someone how they had brought the peonies (which traditionally mean healing and purification) through the holes of the crypt up to the world and the sun. The grieving itself seemed beautiful and healing.

Perhaps the dream was partly inspired by a book called *Crow Planet: Essential Wisdom from the Urban Wilderness* by Lyanda Haupt (2009), from which I copied down a number of passages about consciousness and connections: e.g., "the more we prepare, the more we are 'allowed' somehow to see"; "Writing is a way of seeing. It catches a moment and lends it substance. Writing down an observation gives us a sense of, and a trust in, our own vision." She mentions Rupert Sheldrake's term "morphic resonance," which theorizes "that once an attitude, behavior, or action is 'out there' in the world, it is picked up faster by other organisms." Haupt's book is also filled with many interesting anecdotes about crows: birds I've always admired for their intelligence, scrappiness, and extended families (I used them in my flash poem "Bird

Calls"). In late October, most migratory birds are gone, but the crows stay. Even when the leaves of my favorite tree are nearly gone, the crows on its limb are beautiful, and beauty makes nearly everything a little bit easier.

That fall, I was such a conscientious student in my audited Italian class that it never occurred to me to cut class until one day I did! Playing hooky gave me an extra 75 minutes of practice time, which felt so good since I really needed to work on the difficult rhythms in Levin's work and the fingering in Bach's fugue! (My new teacher, Stefanie, helped me to make Bach SING, whereas Aaron had mainly taught him as a mechanical puzzle.) Playing hooky improved my mood immediately. I could now choose how to spend my time and didn't have to do *everything well*. Later in the day, my diving teacher gave me more pointers. When I was able to integrate her corrections, she said it was my best dive ever—also mood improving!

Still it was hard to believe that just doing what I loved to do was enough. When an acquaintance stopped me to say that she loved my poetry, which she had found at a local bookstore, I was pleased, but embarrassed by her praise at the same time. Similarly, I didn't "count" as "worthwhile" the work I did at Marquette because I was being paid for it. So, apparently I believed that the only thing that "counted" was work I disliked and which I did for free. What was I thinking?

I agreed to visit my acquaintance's poetry group. I thought about giving another recital of work by contemporary women composers. And of course, publishing another book of poetry (*Ties that Bind* was published in 2006 by Finishing Line Press). Some of my ambitions were curtailed, however, by problems with high cholesterol, dizzy spells and headaches, migraine auras, and arthritis in my thumb joints. Yet I felt lucky that I could still do what I did (my cataract surgery had been successful).

A new book by David Shenk called *The Genius in All of Us: Why Everything You've Been Told about Genetics, Talent, and IQ is Wrong* (2010) led me to agree with his conclusion that "how to be a genius" at anything is mainly practice:

> *Whatever you wish to do well, you must do over and over again, in a manner involving repeated attempts to reach beyond one's current level which results in frequent failures. This is known as 'deliberate practice' and over time it can actually produce changes in the brain, making new heights of achievement possible. ... You have to want it, want it so bad you will never give up, so bad that you are ready to sacrifice time, money, sleep, friendships, even your reputation; you have to want it so bad that you are not only ready to fail, but you actually want to experience failure: revel in it, learn from it.*

This struck a responsive chord in me, for I had always told my students the same thing about writing, and had actually written a poem, "directions for playing" (see above, Chapter Twelve) which is about the same phenomenon as it applies to both swimming and piano. On the other hand, Schenk never said where this drive and ambition comes from: Beethoven rewriting a single phrase sixty times, or Ted Williams hitting practice pitches until his hands bled. Perhaps it depends on how much of your life you're willing to give up in order to practice something so intensely. Apparently neither Beethoven nor Williams had very satisfying personal lives outside of their work. For me, I think, the drive came, as always, from glimpsing possibilities and wanting badly to make them into realities. But what if you don't see those possibilities in your environment? I thought again of the fourth-graders in Milwaukee with some of the lowest literacy rates in America, and of Walter Mosley's character, Leonid, in *The Thrill is Gone* (2011). He comes to forgive his Communist father for his poor parenting because, he says, "sometimes a person dreams a dream so vast that, like the ocean, it can drown him." But where do dreams come from? First, you have to see them as possible.

During this same time I had a "night" dream about Angela and Jamie (who had died in 2008) in which I ask them about the meaning of life. Their eyes, comically, go blank with comic-book "x's" on them. They tell me that "meaning" is not the right question. Someone then takes my hand and leads me into a circle of others, chanting the famous lines by Julian of Norwich: "And all things shall be well; all manner of things shall be well."

Is meaning then linked to time? In a 2009 book about time called *From Eternity to Here*, a physicist, Frank Viola, addresses the question of why time appears to go only in one direction. He cites a theory linking it to the entropy following the Big Bang: i.e., that constantly decreasing energy keeps the future constantly "away." Given his theory, time travel would be impossible. The world seems so miraculous to me that it could not possibly be strictly linear. Intuitively, I believe that time loops and breaks apart and reconnects in ways we can barely imagine.

I had always loved reading Madeleine L'Engle's "Time Quintet" novels to my daughters when they were children, including *A Wrinkle in Time* and others, in which one of her characters, a child named Charles Wallace, is able to go back in time to save people important to him and to the world. Of course, given my history, this was also my hope: that actions in the present could affect the past—if not change it, then heal it.

About the same "time" I dreamed of reading a poem called "The Composer," which itself was "composed" (literally, "put together") in a nonlinear way. Part was a letter to one of our daughters about healing. The letter contained a lot of footnotes which I elected not to read because they made the letter very nonlinear. At first I was talking to myself in a narrow hall, far away from the audience. Then I moved to the front of the assembled group, where Ben started to recite the letter with me. Later in the dream I looked at the moon through spring branches and wished that everyone everywhere could have the chance to feel such happiness. Then I glanced over to see a young black man with dreadlocks looking up at the moon as well.

I have come to believe that we make our own meaning and share it with others, who also have voices and their own evolving stories. At times I feel strongly that we can affect the past by changing the way we relate to it. We are separate and not separate. It also occurred to me that the manuscript of poems I was seeking to place was just about that—how life is a dance of connecting and separating. Our marriage had been like that, and now I saw that as *normal*. I felt blessed by such dreams and was inspired to write a poem with footnotes (the old-fashioned kind) that eventually became nothing BUT footnotes. It might have been done before, but perhaps I was just remembering something that hadn't yet been created.

The Craft

The lyf so short, the craft so long to lerne—Geoffrey Chaucer

Meaning arrives slowly,
a song from great distance,
a breeze passing over
ditch water. While it lasts,
you lean into its shiver.

You do not master a craft;
it brushes you with surprise.
And if you tender the tips of
your most hopeless longing,
your most stubborn faults,

craft will bind them into a beauty
so dense, so pure, so rare, so common,
you will find yourself cast into a spell of
amazement and gratitude so deep
you will feel forever young in its thrall.

You do not master a craft;
you are the village fool that fumbles,
falls, breaks the cask: then frees,
attends, willingly surrenders to the genie
everything you have and are:

your seed, your root, your core,
your insatiable need.

Nineteen:

Deconstruction Zone

Julie had some early contractions in late May, 2010, and went into the hospital for a few days. The doctors gave this second baby steroids for the lungs "just in case" he would be premature like his brother. But all seemed to be well, and she went home, though I would return often to help out because Ned had his hands full with Noah, then three. It was a lot of work: cleaning, shopping, cooking, and washing up. I sat in with Julie's appointments with her doula and her obstetrician.

In the midst of all this, I had a few achingly sweet moments with Noah. In one, I was singing to him from the book *Puff the Magic Dragon*, and asked him to sing too. I was treated to the first sound of his sweet little voice as he cut his eyes at me and sang "in the land of Hanalei." And then in late afternoon as Julie was working from home, he and I went to watch the construction work on the street near him. We sat down on the grass right near to where a man with a forklift and bulldozer was off-loading a large number of sewer pipes from a flat-bed truck, driven by another man who guided him through it. It really was pretty interesting, and the men waved and smiled at Noah and let him touch the 'dozer. When Noah thought the action was getting a bit too close, he crawled onto my lap. What a sweetheart!

That day was the inspiration for my one and only children's book, *Deconstruction Zone,* eventually illustrated by local art student Lillian Duermeier.

Noah was such a delight, settling his bears in the front of his little wagon so they could see over the edge while he pulled it to the park in his railroad engineer hat. It took us a long time to get to the playground, but we saw a lot of things on the way: a man flying a kite; guys playing baseball; sticks, seeds, marks on the sidewalk; kids riding bikes; tulips, daffodils, and pansies. Sometimes, characteristically, I would get a bit impatient and walk on ahead, but then he would sing out "I'm coming" and run to catch up, the wagon rattling behind him.

Julie was already feeling what she thought of as the loss of him when this new baby would grow big enough to limit her ability to play with Noah. This was both true and not true, I knew, but she'd have to discover that on her own.

Julie was due to deliver any time. Back home, I finished my second knitted baby blanket and pinned it to a bedspread to be blocked. It looked as good as my sewing projects usually did. Rebecca would arrive soon. All seemed well, but I found myself waking up dreading most days, though they usually turned out fine. It was probably anxiety about the baby's delivery. My wedding ring broke, so I immediately (and somewhat superstitiously) got it fixed: polished and shiny and strengthened with gold solder. Amid all the planning and waiting, Ben and I did manage to take one day out of town to go to a nearby art fair and eat at a new restaurant.

Respite also came in the form of long walks at the dog park with our dog, Elliot. One afternoon I saw two hawks playing with a thermal, and then, flying right across our path, a great blue heron (for me a symbol of poetry which I had tattooed on my left shoulder as a gift to myself when I retired). It landed on a somewhat flimsy-looking shrub and sat for a few minutes only a few feet away. I watched while it looked about before taking off again, very silently. The park was also in its July glory: filled with wild flowers: Queen Anne's lace, chicory, purple clover. I found myself reciting the 23rd Psalm.

Grandson Jason was born, full-term, in late July. All went well despite being a difficult and dramatic delivery. I went to Madison for a week to help out, a general dogs-body for everyone. Julie was so tired yet struggling to breastfeed. I tried to anticipate needs and smooth everyone's way as best I could. Jason's other grandparents took Noah for a few days to play with his cousins, which gave everyone a breather and allowed a predictable schedule.

Rebecca's visit from Europe, where she now lived, was wonderful, and we grasped what few free moments we had in common to talk and catch up. Some mornings, she, Elliot, and I were able to have a leisurely breakfast on the back deck. Someone once commented to me on how different our three daughters seemed to be. It's somewhat true, but that makes it possible for me to relate to different aspects of myself with each of them. I believe that, despite all our differences, we are a close-knit family. For instance, one of my friends never told her mother about her own breast cancer and was surprised that *I* was surprised when she did *not*. I can't imagine any of my own daughters keeping a secret of that magnitude from me, but perhaps that's naïve. I would certainly have hesitated to tell *my* mother. Nevertheless, I knew that Julie would find her way with each of her two very different sons.

Finally, I had a chance to dive for the first time in nearly two months. I felt quite rusty and was therefore surprised when an older woman said it was a "joy" to watch me. I registered the effect that her comment had had on my mood and vowed to "appreciate" others' actions more openly, for I believe we don't do it nearly enough. I also began piano lessons again in early September, starting some variations by Schoenberg. Rhythm, as always, is tricky for me. I can usually imitate a rhythm if I hear it first, but counting out a bar of 32^{nds} without having heard it first is a challenge. I planned a recital at the conservatory for the following June, finding it hard to believe that it had been five years since the last one. Ben and I kept attending occasional symphonies, and I especially enjoyed one with a work by Gabriel Fauré, written in his 70s after he had fallen ill. The creative impulse keeps on to the end, or so it seems, if one does not become too distracted or limited by other things.

While paying bills, I realized, once again, that as a family we were falling behind our financial goals, mainly because we constantly underestimated how much things actually cost: the various components of our long-postponed trip to Italy; a new set of family portraits; eating out; the rising cost of gas, food, and prescription drugs, and the amount of all of them we used. Similarly, I vastly underestimated how much some badly-needed new windows would cost, which would have to be put off, despite the extra fuel it would cost to heat our one-hundred-year-old house in winter.

But life went on. The weather took a warm turn after the week-long cold snap that came in early September. My sailing partner and I did go sailing one day, but there was no wind—just strong waves that kept pushing us back in. I tried to rig the sail myself before she got there but just ended up messing up the jib sheet, for which we paid later. But in the process of making mistakes, as always, I learned something. A few days later, we went sailing in heavy air—reefed the mainsail by ourselves, successfully "rescued" the life-preserver from the water several times, and were generally quite proud of ourselves!

I switched my yoga class to Saturday so I could make up most of the summer classes I'd missed. Both my yoga and piano teachers provided lessons for my own teaching. I continued to appreciate their kindness, approachability, standards, and the fact that they give my process so much individual attention.

Laney and I occasionally cooked together since we were often alone in the house. She had some trouble adjusting to the discipline of studying again, but made a good effort, eventually becoming a lawyer. She drove me to the auto-repair to have a side-mirror fixed and painted and we had a good talk over coffee and hot chocolate on the way back. She wanted to switch beds with Rebecca, which I thought was fair, but which Rebecca would probably hate. Thinking of Julie and her two new sons, I reflected on the difficulties of attending to each child's needs, especially when they seem to conflict.

Small things can lift a mood: finding a pen refill in a world of disposables and thus giving new life to a favorite pen; being able to help a friend with the draft of a poem; making some household calls I'd been putting off and finding that they went more easily than I'd feared; a personal "best" at the pool; seeing steady improvement in the Joan Tower and Ruth Crawford pieces planned for my recital. All such things helped to counter worries about money, friends, and family. I longed for "still time," which September weather usually brings—a fleeting beauty, but one that reminded me there was "still" time to do most of the things I wanted to do, even into my late 60s, inspiring a poem by that name. I saw a hanging cluster of monarchs in the local park one morning walking Elliot, and later at the dog park, a "kettle" of about ten hawks flying round and round as they prepared themselves for migration.

Ben took a fall on his bike and had to have stitches; my arthritic thumb still hurt. We were both dealing with our own physical and internal issues and had to remember to be kind and patient with each other. Despite the thumb pain, the hand doctor didn't recommend surgery, so I just had to put up with it. I chose a lot of music for left-hand only, which presented a whole new challenge. I hoped to play some of it at our first adult piano student "get-together" in November. Because I didn't have to have surgery, I was free to read my prize-winning poems in Madison. Julie and her mother-in-law attended, as well as Noah, Jason, Ned, and Laney, which was nice.

I spent a day and night in Madison, able to catch up with Julie and Ned and my grandsons. Then I drove a little farther to attend a Full Moon Circle with Selena. I didn't know anyone there but Selena, but I needed the solitude and time to look inward and to send out blessings for others. I had plenty of names to offer, all of whom were facing different, but equally difficult, challenges and adjustments.

Julie was discovering that staying home all day with two young children was NOT a vacation, and she felt guilty when she was stressed and snapped at Noah. I reminded her that I had snapped at her around that same age even though I didn't have a newborn also vying for my undivided attention. Luckily, she didn't even remember. Noah, at three, was needy, didn't like his new school, and had nightmares. One morning while there, I took Noah to his pre-school. He said he didn't want to go but didn't kick and scream as he'd done for Julie. He just whispered, "I'll miss you, Grandma" and then wouldn't look at me when I did what I knew I had to: turn away, leave.

Sit. Stay.

In yoga, holding Virasana, thighs trembling,
I think of how my pup learned to "stay"
during his second Doggie Manners class.

He wanted so badly *not* to "stay," wanted to
bound up and explore the butt of the aspirant
panting placidly on the next mat.

The only way he *could* "stay" was by looking
up at the ceiling. He still trembled, but for a
moment I felt the room fade, with its twelve dogs

and their disciples, as his practice elevated
us both before he glanced down, broke form.
Learning how to live in the world without

a leash might someday save his life.
Today as I lean back into Ustrasana,
a strap binds my ankles, but someday I may be

able to let it fall. Some day
I may even untether my breath from thought,
leaving me space to curb pain and fear.

                                    But now,
gripping the ceiling with my eyes, I think:

This is basic. This is crucial. This is
the hardest thing I have ever done.

Twenty:

Heidegger and a Hippo Walk through the Pearly Gates

In the fall, while in Milwaukee for Ben's birthday, Noah helped me rake leaves, and Jason won me over by spitting out his pacifier and grinning when he visited our home for the first time.

I started teaching a new class at Marquette with six returning adult students, even though I felt myself getting sick. Then, realizing that my discomfort was nothing next to those suffering from the huge cholera epidemic in Haiti, the questions started again: why were some people so much luckier than others? what was the best way to spend whatever time I had left? as we make way for new generations, what can we do, clearly, cleanly in the present? do we just continue the arcs begun long ago, living in some universe parallel to the new ones popping up around us every day? I did sometimes miss the once-familiar, youthful world in which we all had once existed. Many of those I knew were now dead, and yet we went on. We created family and worked to reconcile ourselves with the past. Perhaps that's what matters after all else is gone.

After Thanksgiving and before Christmas, I took a day to "go to the well"—to the country, to Lizard Mound. Though it was roped off for the season, that did not keep me from walking in. I was completely alone, which was my desire. It was snowing a bit, and the colors of fall were heightened and softened at the same time. All was grey, brown, pale yellow, silver. There were a few red berries, bluebirds. As I climbed the fence to sit in the back field, everything stilled. When my legs got tired in "hero's pose," I lay flat on my back and let the snow blink on my eyelids. I was completely open with gratitude to the great solitude which is not solitude at all.

I found myself giving true thanks and asking for ways to give more out of the best of what I am. Answers came, but not new ones: Do not seek to be a grand giver. Trust that small gifts matter. The beauty of the hills is "of use." Each snowflake is "of use" in its uniqueness, but also as it links with others to seed the earth with snow. Be who you are; everyone else is taken. You will not be asked why you were not Mahatma Gandhi or Mother Theresa. Bloom where you are planted. Make something nourishing from what is already at hand. I continued to foster the young when I could, to give when I was asked, to write to my new *Women for Women International* 18-year-old "sister" in Afghanistan and pray for the one who could no longer come safely to the program, for the one whose husband and father cut off her nose and ears because she sought to escape from abuse. Teach. Write. Play: these were the things that gave me joy and which were the best I had to offer. Even meager gifts can be of use, as the *I Ching* repeatedly says. Together, the members of my writing group gave a reading in February to benefit a food pantry.

I started Brian Greene's latest book, *The Hidden Reality* (2011), about current theories regarding parallel lives. Though intriguing in the same way that Jane Roberts' books were thirty-five years ago, the current theories seemed to me soulless and somewhat terrifying—such a plethora of branching selves that the idea of meaningful choice and the significance of any one life seemed threatened. It roused the same feeling I had in early adolescence when I first became aware of the universe and my tiny place in it. A recurrent terrifying image was being literally "lost in space," completely alone, with no ground to stand on.

A concurrent article in the *New York Times* stated that most scientists of all kinds no longer believe in free will, yet all cultures need the belief in order to thrive. It's said to be one of those traits/beliefs that furthers the good of society as well as individual well-being. So I come back to Wallace Stevens' "supreme fiction" once again: the choice to act "as if" something is "true," knowing that it is a "fiction": a created construction of meaning.

A novel, *The London Train* (2011), by Tessa Hadley, offered these insights into such conundrums:

> *We've subjected religious beliefs to the wrong kind of scrutiny as if they needed to be true in a scientific sense. So we're desolated by our cleverness in an empty universe. We need the symbols and stories that embody the idea of another dimension, beyond the one we actually inhabit. But just because we need them, that doesn't make them true. Maybe there isn't any other dimension. No: the fact that we need them is what makes them true. We bring that dimension into existence, our imagination in creative collaboration with the life-forces outside us and the mysteries of physics, which otherwise have no outlet for being known. Those forces are incomplete without our faith as we're incomplete without their existence beyond us.*

And then, this, which brought me closer to what was actually happening in my life:

She had tried to treasure up relics from every phase of her life as it passed, as if they were holy. Now that seemed to be a falsely consoling model of experience. The present was always paramount, in a way that thrust you forward: empty, but also free. Whatever stories you told over to yourself and others, you were in truth exposed and naked in the present, a prow cleaving new waters; your past was insubstantial, behind, it fell away, it grew into desuetude, its forms grew obsolete. The problem was, you were always still alive, until the end. You had to do something.

Indeed. And so I put down the book and turned to immediate conundrums. Nevertheless, one needs diversions as one deals with the detritus of the past and turns to face an unknown future. I thought that maybe the key to my uneasiness was to act "as if" this were the only life that counts and that what I choose to do actually matters. A book by a Canadian woman—Marina Endicott—called *Good to a Fault* (2008) is an interesting look at how "doing good" is not at odds with doing what one loves to do. It highlights how often we believe that it only "counts" if such work is unpleasant. So I'm apparently not the only one with this damaging belief.

* * *

In March of 2011, I turned 66, a "respectable number of years," as one of my younger friends said. I made a list of wishes, seeing no particular reason to limit myself to only one:

- that my thumb would improve and not get in the way of the piano
- that Ben would find a way to approach his work that would relieve his stress
- that our daughters and grandchildren would be happy and healthy
- that Ben and I would enjoy healthy old ages together

233

- that I would find ways of "giving back" that make use of the very best parts of me
- that I could finally come to peace regarding the loss of my sister
- that I could come to understand more about the universe in a way that doesn't freak me out
- that I would continue to grow in balance and whatever is meant by wisdom.

I realized even then that that was a lot to ask for, but can report after six years that most of my wishes have come true. Probably, it's been said, we never ask for enough.

I prepared a new chapbook manuscript called *Rescue Mission*, which is pretty dark—about the connections between death and art. I realized, putting it together, that my thoughts about death had changed over the years. The belief in reincarnation (at least as usually defined) had faded. Despite the possibility of parallel lives, which actually frightened me, this life was IT. My hope was to die before I became too ill to enjoy life, though I suppose, like everything, there would be lessons in that, as well. For someone. But at 66 I felt well-acquainted with death, at least the death of others, but of course, not yet my own. It is, as someone once said, "the last surprise."

I did have a kind of "passage" dream of my own. I knew I was going to die, so I was saying goodbye to relatives such as my aunt and uncle and then my mother, who smiled at me as if the insights I had had about her youth had made a difference. I was aware of "crossing over" a river and pumping the air, happy because I had done all that I was supposed to have done. My life was, in every sense, complete.

Julie also told me of a numinous dream about Jamie "making amends" by operating surgically on Jason to remove the possibility of colon cancer (of which Jamie had died). She/Jamie were aware of each other's presence, but couldn't look at or acknowledge each other. Her dream apparently sparked a dream in me. I was in a large circle of friends and relatives outside, celebrating something when I felt Jamie's presence behind me. As the celebration came to an end, I turned toward a nearby tree and looked up; hanging on the branches were mementos of the best of our times together— the books we'd read, the trips we'd taken, gifts I'd given him which were being given back to me, along with the message "Don't forget to look up."

I kept sending out the manuscript for my new chapbook, *Rescue Mission*, which was finally accepted by a small press in Connecticut (Antrim House, 2011). As a bonus, the artist of an Orpheus/Eurydice print I admire, Leslie Xuereb, agreed to let me use the image for the book cover for free. The image inspired me to write another poem for the book—one about Orpheus. The poet and essayist Jane Hirshfield contributes these thoughts about the Orpheus myth:

> *Orpheus's loss of Eurydice remains both the story of a heartbreaking surrender to human weakness and a clue— the true musician is the one who sings on, after the second loss. Even when music is powerless, even when it includes failure and shame as well as grief, he sings. Feeling what cannot be borne, he sings. Amidst and past his own dying, he sings.* (Ten Windows: How Great Poems Transform the World, 2015)

Yes: "Even when music is powerless, even when it includes failure and shame as well as grief, he sings." Unfortunately, as Lewis Hyde would lament, and as is apparently the indie publishing practice these days, though Antrim Press did a great job with *Rescue Mission*, and I enjoyed working with the editor enormously, our family had to pick up the tab for a run of 300 copies before even one could be sold. Supposedly we would double that investment if I sold all 300 copies for $13/each, but of course I never did. I tried to set up a website for marketing the book, but it proved to be more complicated than I'd anticipated. I still have boxes of them in my closet even after giving many away. I don't think that my experience is unique, which is why I finally turned to print-on-demand services.

The reading for my "book release" went well. Members of my writing group were very supportive in getting people there. I recorded it and put segments on You Tube, which was an interesting, if frustrating, process. *Deconstruction Zone* was out by December as well—more for me to peddle. By November I was giving the books away, which made me again struggle with the fear that what I'd done so far in my life hadn't amounted to much. Despite my best attempts to make my "art" matter to anyone other than me, it hadn't seemed to. I'd received a few nice comments, but despite my efforts to make my music and poetry be about more than just me, I didn't believe I had. Unexpectedly, however, a neighbor who came to my book release asked me to be her paid writing coach, to which I readily agreed, starting a new "career" which continues and which I love.

*   *   *

Christmas came and went. I found myself more and more conscious of how fast my life was passing. I was sad that so relatively little time was left. This was reinforced when my favorite aunt fell and had to go into a nursing home. But Ben cheered me up with a book he got me for Christmas: *Heidegger and a Hippo Walk through the Pearly Gates.* It made me laugh. Here's the title joke:

> *Heidegger and the hippo stroll up to the pearly gates and Saint Peter says, listen, we've only got room for one more today. So, whoever of the two of you gives me the best answer to the question: What is the meaning of life - gets to come in.*
>
> *And Heidegger says, to think being itself explicitly requires disregarding being to the extent that it is only grounded and interpreted in terms of beings and for beings as their ground as in all metaphysics.*

But before the hippo can grunt one word, Saint Peter says to him, today's your lucky day, hippy.

In the New Year, Ben and I had some time alone over our anniversary in Door County. I found a nice place for us, and the snow made it seem reminiscent of our honeymoon trip there 28 years past. We did go on rather long hikes in Peninsula State Park. We had some nice meals and even a couples' massage, which Ben insisted he had enjoyed.

Relaxed, I was able to list all the things I enjoy, including being around him doing all the things we've always enjoyed; laughing with Rebecca; talking poetry with Laney; having deep conversation with Julie; playing with Noah and Jason. And, alone, doing yoga, having lunch out, practicing the piano, reading the NYT on Sunday and women-authored mysteries at night, walks, swimming, friends, creating as much order, beauty, and awareness in and around me as I could. Life was rich, and I was grateful. At the same time I realized that all was temporary, that structures were loosening and would gradually shift.

My first online class for the returning-adult students at Marquette went all right; nevertheless, the unreliability of the technology made me nervous. We met online every other week, so I had already met the twelve nice, engaging people the week before. The class did make me aware of a growing hearing loss, however: I had to ask several people to repeat what they had said, several times.

My hearing loss was also probably affecting my piano playing, as I really needed to work to increase my range of dynamics. I attended a master class by Joyce Yang, who was a real inspiration. I also listened to some recordings of the works I was practicing, such as a Bach Prelude. We were getting into the fine nuances of expression (Stefanie would not find them "fine"), but it was largely unexplored territory for me, and I didn't want to lose my hearing just as I was really beginning to study the fine points of performance dynamics. Meanwhile, I ordered some music from an American composer named Elizabeth R. Austin—a sonata that alternates piano and poetry. Exciting.

I also began to realize how hard-of-hearing people can easily become more and more isolated from what is going on around them. Television was becoming hard to understand: the voices themselves were garbled, no matter how loud. A hearing test showed that my hearing, especially in my left ear, had deteriorated. Hearing aids cost $6K per pair, though our current health insurance would pay one-third.

Though teaching classes presented hearing challenges, working one-to-one with a poetry client was entirely do-able. Soon others asked me to work with me, and they all seemed to bloom through our work together, which was immensely satisfying to me. Perhaps, I thought, my ways of being "helpful" were starting to present themselves all on their own.

I was also asked, out of the blue, to do a writing workshop for an wealthy suburban elementary school. Ordinarily, I would not have done it because I had no experience teaching groups of small children; however, it paid a lot of money, which we needed. I had about two months to create a detailed preparation after talking with the school organizers. I decided to choose the theme of endangered animals around the world as a focus for the fourth and fifth graders' writing. This was in keeping with the celebration of "Earth Day" in April, when the workshop would take place. All went well except that worried parents complained about how the "realities" of vanishing species had adversely affected their children's sense of well-being.

My current well-being seemed dependent upon doing something about how my issues with my past had become enmeshed in current issues with my own daughters. Perhaps we are all carrying "wounded children" around inside of us that we unconsciously try to protect. I definitely needed to find a healthy way to relate to myself and my grown daughters as adults. My inner work regarding my issues remained right up front, in my face, as my daughters struggled with their own lives. And even when there were no crises of epic proportions,

I still had emotional issues, for instance, as I saw Julie disappearing into her own life, with the line of connection still there but less immediate. It was all normal and good, but still aroused feelings of intense loss.

* * *

Meanwhile, another micro-press was interested in my old Baubo poems manuscript, *Avatars of Baubo*, written between '94 and '98, for their "grandmother" imprint. With some editing and additional artwork, it would come out the following year. The press was run by a cooperative, which interested me (Green Fuse Poetic Arts, 2013). On the other hand, my poem, "Wild Rhubarb" was rejected by *Penumbra*, but the editor wrote a really nice note saying it had made the final round; it just hadn't fit well with the other pieces selected. More editors should realize what a difference the form of their rejection makes! Our group hadn't been meeting frequently enough for me to get any feedback, so I tended to send out poems too early, blinded by what a fellow poet aptly calls "puppy love." Some of them, though, were just older poems I'd never placed, but had reworked. In the meantime, I read Sharon Olds' new *Stag Leap*, about her divorce, which was as riveting as a novel. She is so good, turning this way and that the emotional experience of being abandoned, using amazing language and cadences in the process.

I came down with a respiratory illness that, as usual, lasted and lasted, seeping my energy away, and forcing me to cut back on my many activities. And with that, as always, my mood plummeted, but gradually, the huge, heavy engine of my life began to move forward again, bit by bit. Loving attention from Ben on the weekends lifted my spirits as well. He accepted the offer of another year of consulting work in Iowa, though more of that would be from home, which I appreciated. I looked forward to the easier give and take that came with everyday contact. It bothered me that I was still so vulnerable to being "left": being alone, especially when I'm not at my best physically. But more and more I seemed to come to accept my vulnerabilities as part of the human condition and not necessarily situations that have to be "learned from" or overcome. I didn't know if that was a healthy view, but it seemed to be where I was headed. Maybe it's just a factor of getting older. The "inner child" exercises also seemed to help. I could see myself go from being snippy and irritable to more relaxed and generous within a single day. My therapist reassured me with the surprising notion that sadness isn't necessarily pathological (depression).

Similarly, I sensed a change in my views about meaning and free will—more toward the view that, like all other creatures, we just are who we are: free will doesn't come into it unless it's the freedom to BE what we already are, or have the potential to become. And that "meaning" is little more than the full experience of who we are—that life is already so filled with so much mystery and beauty—a full tableau in which we find ourselves—that there's no need to struggle to make it more than it already is. Again, I suspect that this view is another consequence of MY unfolding: i.e., getting older. I do feel incredibly lucky, like that hippo.

I asked myself about my priorities—where are my sails set? Family and friends seemed more clearly at the top than earlier in my life, when ego and achievement were foremost. I no longer believed that my gifts would be of great use to the world, nor did I worry about it very much. Given the ripple effect, one never knows, and so, ignorant, I continue to offer what I can give out of my talents and interests, even in small measure. Over and over the *I Ching* tells me that the sentiments of the heart can be expressed even with meager gifts. And so I continue to practice nearly every day, which is treatment for my own anxiety and depression, as I plan a recital for summer, hopefully to bring some modicum of joy and interest and beauty to others. And I rejoiced when *Avatars of Baubo* came out as a chapbook, even though I knew it would not travel very far. But perhaps it would make someone laugh, or think, or feel seen for a moment.

*   *   *

Jim Harrison's novellas *The River Swimmer* (2004) came at a good time for me. I copied some passages: "Once you reach sixty, you had to kill your ego so that you wouldn't become desperately unhappy about disappearing in your old age," and "He should just paint and then the doors of the world are surprisingly open if you don't lock them," and "His oldest and best teacher had advised him not to say [that] things were impossible in a universe with ninety billion galaxies. Einstein had said that it's not for scientists to drill holes in a thin piece of board. All mysteries must be explored." All good advice for those of us edging toward seventy. Harrison himself died at the age of 69 in 2016.

I received no prize in the state poetry contest that year. I had suspected that I wouldn't because there were at least three times the number of entries as before. It is sometimes hard, as Leonard Cohen has suggested, to honor one's own work, despite its reception, despite how "good" or "bad" it's judged to be. I held fast to that point when, again, I received no piano scholarship money for the following year. There were five contestants that year, not just our usual three. I wondered whether to continue to compete, even though I always need some event to prepare for to keep me sharp—and I can't prepare a solo recital every year. But I continued to prepare for the recital that year.

Some of my adult students at Marquette believed that I was holding them to too high of a standard in my expectations for their online postings. Yet there were others who appreciated the standards which gave them the opportunity to revise. One of these thanked me and said that I had a reputation for being the kind of teacher who's hard, but from whom you'll learn a lot. I was surprised at how good it felt to get that little bit of appreciation for doing a job for which I've never felt very valued.

Self-doubt is insidious. I wish I could just accept everything I do with the same attitude I bring to yoga. I know I will never be great at it, but doing it is better than not doing it.

Maybe inspired by my grandsons, I had a happy dream of childhood, holding hands with one of my cousins and jumping through unplowed snowdrifts. Then I returned to a sorority at Circle, where many "sisters" welcomed me as if I had been gone a long time. They made much of me, doing my hair, etc. I was so happy.

The feeling faded to nostalgia and sadness as the day went on. Spring recalls childhood—happy days before the world widened and changed: when the earth and grass and flowers and sky and animals were enough. I visited the small garden at Hope House (a homeless shelter where my service-learning students were once involved) and spent a little time helping with that. I remember my therapist's point that sorrow about the past can be seductive; that I've dealt (*ad infinitum*) with the issues about my past and that I should try to unhitch those experiences from my current issues, renegotiating relationships as things and circumstances change. Good advice, but I would have to hear it again and again before it started to happen.

It didn't help that my recital was only twelve days away. Things were coming together, but I have a history of anxiety there too, which I also needed to deal with. Ben knew how stressed I had been and took pains to make things easier for me, at least physically.

I enjoyed preparing the program notes, the refreshments, deciding on clothes, etc. I decided to depend on the printed music for all of the pieces, and with the relief of not having to memorize, my anxiety level came way down. Together, a close friend and I practiced the spoken and played sections of Elizabeth R. Austin's "Rose Sonata" at the conservatory. I ordered seven dozen mini-cupcakes with frosting roses and found someone to record it for a reasonable price. All in all, plus rental of the hall, it cost me $300 with a possible return of $100 or so for the library.

The recital itself, with the presence of so many loving family and friends, I considered "glorious," despite the occasional cracks and dings in my playing. Jason and Noah were both there, which was extra special. Laney and Ben were great helps in taking care of tasks so that I could focus on what I needed to. Elizabeth R. Austin sent me flowers, as did Stefanie, and other friends. I made $90 for the conservatory's holdings of scores by women. The comments afterwards meant so much. One said that the recital was the "highlight of her summer." Another said that she and others took turns reading poems about roses afterwards.

* * *

As the glow of the recital slowly and inevitably faded into the past, the tasks and issues of everyday life necessarily returned to be taken up once again. My life felt busy—even crowded—but very little time involved Ben. Given that so many of my friends' husbands were dying or were facing life-threatening issues, I longed for more time together. We still struggled to find the time to connect. Meanwhile, I continued to work on my own issues with my therapist, kept up my many and various friendships, kept tabs on our children, as I took up new challenges with music and poetry. "Wild Rhubarb" was finally accepted, with some revision, by *Future Cycle*'s new anthology of poems in honor of Malala Yousafzai and her growing activist work for the education of women everywhere. I felt both honored and humbled to be included in a hundred-page anthology with the likes of Jane Hirshfield and Ellen Bass!

Rebecca came for a three-week visit, which is always fun. We went for a beautiful sail and made dinner together. She helped out with Elliot, as well, and found some time to go horseback riding. She was doing well and had recently found a flat of women her age to live with in London. She was to have a floor under the eaves with a large bedroom and study of her own to write in.

My "empty nest" and health issues triggered a bout of de-cluttering and cleaning up "under the eaves" in our house. I found several letters that moved me while cleaning out old boxes. One was by my favorite aunt from '92 about our family history; another was a letter I wrote to my daughters in '88 as a part of a "Death and Dying" course for my MSW, and finally a late poem/letter from Angela in spring of '97, when she was obviously suffering a lot, losing it, but at the same time trying to tell me how much she cared. That one I had forgotten, and it made me cry.

There are still so many old letters and photos—most of which I never want to read or look at again because they can suck me right back into the past—but I did sort the letters into Ziploc bags by writer, and tried to protect the photos in the same way. The rest will be up to the girls. Still, it felt good to clean, organize, and shift places in the house that had remained the same for years. It made room for the new, although it also felt a little like dying: like saying goodbye to most of my past. So I tried once again to keep my balance, doing some self-talk, realizing that I could both bear the weight of and continue to transform my past, just as I could clear space for more deliberate choices about the future. This would be even more important in the coming months, as my therapist was retiring for health reasons at the end of the month. Her announcement made perfect sense, but I still started to cry, which wasn't really fair to her. I seemed to be crying a lot, which was unusual for me and maybe not that bad.

I went back to Kansas in October of 2013 for my 50th high school reunion and to visit relatives. I took a pot of chrysanthemums to the cemetery along with wire hooks to hold it down in the 30 mph wind. I added some remembrance pebbles to what I had left there the previous December, splashed water also on the gravestones for renewal, and then talked a little to my dad, mom, and Marilyn, falling into unexpected tears at her grave. But even that felt healing, and I didn't need to linger. It felt good to have lived long enough to bring some peace to situations that had always been so painful.

Returning home, I picked up the threads of my many connections, and Ben and I made a concerted effort not to just lead separate lives. Often at night I woke with anxiety that kicked in immediately if I couldn't go right back to sleep. I worried about whether I'd be alive in ten years, and if so, in what state. I worried about being alone and without enough money; I worried about our daughters; and then I ranged wider and started worrying about those out in the extreme cold last night (people and animals), and then the polar bears, whose habitat is vanishing. At some point I reminded myself that fear only shuts down possibility and makes no room for the unexpected, or for laughter. But usually these realizations are not much help at 4:45 a.m. Winter solstice, the "lost heart of Christmas," as I call it, came and went unnoticed. Yet people everywhere at the start of winter seem to need the reminder that the light is not going away forever: that, in fact, even if indiscernible, it has started to return.

In the morning, I thought once again of a poem by the seventeenth-century English poet, George Herbert. In "The Flower" he remarks on the difference between his night fears and his joy in the morning:

How Fresh, O Lord, how sweet and clean
Are thy returns! ev'n as the flowers in spring;

To which, besides their own demean,
The late-past frosts tributes of pleasure bring.
Grief melts away
Like snow in May,
As if there were no such cold thing.

Who would have thought my shrivel'd heart
Could have recover'd greennesse? It was gone
Quite under ground; as flowers depart

245

To see their mother-root, when they have blown;
Where they together
All the hard weather,
Dead to the world, keep house unknown.

These are thy wonders, Lord of power,
Killing and quickning, bringing down to hell
And up to heaven in an houre;
Making a chiming of a passing-bell,
We say amisse,
This or that is:
Thy word is all, if we could spell.

O that I once past changing were;
Fast in thy Paradise, where no flower can wither!
Many a spring I shoot up fair,
Offring at heav'n, growing and groning thither:
Nor doth my flower
Want a spring-showre,
My sinnes and I joining together;

But while I grow to a straight line;
Still upwards bent, as if heav'n were mine own,
Thy anger comes, and I decline:
What frost to that? what pole is not the zone,
Where all things burn,
When thou dost turn,
And the least frown of thine is shown?

And now in age I bud again,
After so many deaths I live and write;
I once more smell the dew and rain,
And relish versing: O my onely light,
It cannot be
That I am he
On whom thy tempests fell all night.

These are thy wonders, Lord of love,
To make us see we are but flowers that glide:
Which when we once can finde and prove,
Thou hast a garden for us, where to bide.
Who would be more,
Swelling through store,
Forfeit their Paradise by their pride.

"And now in age I bud again" are such reassuring words. They remind me that there are so many who came before me who have had to wrestle with the same issues.

Perhaps the point about Heidegger and the Hippo is correct: sometimes we don't even need to open our mouths to receive Grace. Nevertheless, here I offer my own poem about the hope and insights that can accompany age.

At Seventy

At seventy, the thing she wanted
to learn was to dive:

to tuck her chin to her chest, between
her outstretched arms and to fall

headfirst toward the bottom she had both
feared and yearned for since she had

first seen water—the still pool
untouched, unrippled, heavy with meaning

and promise: to feel its cool caress, hear
the bubbles of breath leave her body, see

the illusion of being enclosed utterly by blue;
to know that she could aim her body down,

then up, and it would joyously comply,
her remaining breath buoying her up, up,

up to break the surface of the old familiar
world as if rising from sleep; it was something

like flying, she thought, something like
taking off from one medium and trying on

another, shedding one set of rules for a second:
one which both frightened and enthralled,

a kind of life to which she had always been born,
on the edge of which she has been forever poised.

Twenty-One:

"Hello, Beautiful!"

As our dog Elliot and I were taking our walk one afternoon, a middle-aged man on a bike called, "Hi Beautiful!" as he passed us. The compliment was so unexpected, and I was so surprised and pleased that I laughed out loud! Of course, he could have been talking to Elliot.

But sometimes, as noted in the previous chapter, Grace just happens. In her memoir, *Lab Girl (2017)*, Hope Jahren writes: "I had worked so hard for so many years trying to make my life into something that it was a surprise to see all the truly valuable pieces simply fall from the sky undeserved."

This is not the end; no. But it is the beginning of the end. This book will be published almost exactly two years after Ben received his diagnosis of esophageal cancer. But that was not the end, either. Before that, before the surgery that would eventually be deemed successful, were two years of resolution—not final, of course, because nothing is ever really final.

But there remained issues that I needed to resolve.

All my daughters still seemed to need me; in fact, there was an accusation that I played favorites. It really frustrated me to try to explain why I don't have a "favorite" child. It was true (with my grandsons too) that until I got to know the new child, I always wondered how I could possibly love the next child as much. But I always have. It's a mystery. Or maybe not. When we really get to know someone, there appears a whole new, unique connection between unused parts of ourselves and this new person. It is absolutely true that I have a completely different connection with each child, grandchild, and yes, husband. I don't know how to say it more clearly. Each relationship is unique, intimate, and loving in its never-to-be-repeated way.

Ben and I have come through: have been able to build a life on an equal basis, dancing through to a deeper, more honest intimacy than I have ever had before—with anyone. Now that he is working from home most of the time, things are much more relaxed. We are adjusting to less income as well, but that actually puts us on a more equal footing. There is less discrepancy between the amount of money each of us brings in, and this makes a huge difference to me. Still, it is sometimes hard for both of us to balance time together with needed time alone.

We both have health issues. Still, he brings me laughter and reassurance about the future, though I know he worries too, about money mainly. Worry brings nothing good, but recognition of that fact does not keep it away.

The girls continue with their lives, and we are still involved with theirs as well as our grandsons.' We buy a bigger dining room table to seat our growing family on holidays, so I guess we are not planning to move anytime soon. We re-finance this old house again.

I plan another recital and another book, *The Beautiful Unnamed*, which I decide to self-publish and release at the time of the recital, sometime in June of 2015, shortly after my 70th birthday. I plan to give away donations for the book to an inner-city arts program, and play music from the previous year as well as new music.

Donna Tartt's novel, *The Goldfinch (2015)*, speaks strongly to me about the importance of art. She quotes Nietzsche: "We have art in order not to die from the truth"; and one of her characters asks, "As cruelly as the game is stacked, isn't it possible to play with a kind of joy?" And another adds, "Isn't it better to throw yourself head first and laughing into the holy rage calling your name?" I answer "yes" to both questions.

I am inspired to start a blog which will follow my progress in preparing my recital and my book. Its theme was, like Tartt's, the value of art, but I intended to use many variations on that theme during the nine months of preparation. Though it had only a few readers, I appreciated them, and I enjoyed the process of connecting thought and reading as I have always done in my journals, though this time with an audience who responded. Some accused me of being too long-winded, or of being too forceful in seeking an audience. Nevertheless, I never forget Andy Goldsworthy's message, repeated by a character in Emily Arsenault's novel *Miss Me When I'm Gone*, that "The sound of your love's voice fades and the sad story dies with you, or with the one you told it to. Either way, it disappears. A few will wonder what your story was and then no one will at all. There is a certain beauty in that, isn't there—in how it all disappears?"

"Quivira"—a long poem arising from my last visit to Kansas—was published, much to my delight, as well as the individual poem "The Beautiful Unnamed." I also wrote new poems about a homeless woman who duped me out of $200 on a cold, cold January day, and about my speculations on "safety" and homelessness as I walked back to the parking lot after my new job as a gate-screener at Miller Park.

Unexpectedly I won a prize in the state poetry contest again, for a poem called "The Self-Organizing Universal Nail Salon." They also published "Palimpsest: Painting Her Again," which pleased me. I believed (wrongly) it would be the last poem I would ever write for my sister.

Several old friends approached me spontaneously to be their "mentors"—either for their poetry or, in one case, as a "life coach." Doing this brings me great pleasure, as well as a little income, so I think that, despite all my attempts at finding a way to be "useful," "doing good," a way has actually found *me*. My plan of playing piano for hospice patients didn't pan out—there are apparently no available pianos in hospices! And I had dreaded doing it!

I dreamed that I am a "senior" chosen to represent "Time" in some sort of graduation play. I was flattered; however, Time was introduced as "ugly and fearsome" as opposed to the cooler girls who were supposed to represent Love, etc. The only positive thing I could say in my role was "without me, none of you would exist." I woke up with this riddle: "What is it that we always want more of, but that, in the end, takes everything away?"

I began therapy with still another therapist: not a Jungian, but one who works with Jung's theories, which have always been quite helpful to me. I went for the same reason I have always gone—to get help and insight for my recurrent anxiety and depression. Sometimes my own self-talk—trying to loosen up my own pretensions and certainties about negative things—helps, but I have found it also valuable to have a therapist who 1) doesn't tell me what to do, 2) doesn't talk about her own life, but 3) holds me responsible for my own healing. Feedback, to me, has always been imperative.

Being 70 turned out to be fine, by the way. Of course, we don't feel old unless we are sick, and luckily I feel basically healthy despite my various acute and chronic ailments. My hairdresser had 70 tulips (my favorite flower) delivered on my birthday—such a surprise! I agree with Lee Smith's comment, though, from her memoir *Dimestore: A Writer's*

Life (2017): "I'm seventy, an age that has brought no wisdom. When I was young, I always thought the geezers knew some things I didn't; the sad little secret is, we don't. I don't understand anything anymore, though I'm still in there, still trying like crazy." She adds, "Often I don't even know what I think until I go back and read what I've written. My belief is that we have only one life, that is all there is. And I refuse to lead an unexamined life. No matter how painful it may be, I want to know what's going on."

Such groundlessness will become important in reacting to various mental and physical crises of members of our family in these years. I still worry about everyone in my family, but try to neutralize worry when I can. I can't control anything, nor am I indispensable, nor do I want to be. It is still hard to see my daughters suffer for any reason. I am a "fixer" but they don't need me to do that anymore, nor can I. To merely listen still seems unnatural and hard. My work is to keep steady, support when I can, and not to catastrophize, which is usually a struggle. But that's my present work—responding as the present requires and not as my fears dictate. At one point, a daughter tells me to back off so that she can start relying on herself, not me: that I'm so "efficient" that it makes her feel even more that she can't "do" for herself. Ben says, rather bluntly, that I often hear only what I want to hear and enjoy running other people's lives and telling them what to do. My therapist says, echoing my last one, that my true "shadow" is Powerlessness. I feel stuck between doing everything I can to make sure the person at risk "survives" and taking the risk that she will tough it out on her own. It's hard to find the middle way. But this therapist seemed to have arrived in my life at a good time. The trick, as in yoga, is to hold one's anxiety at bay, enduring it while things are working themselves out. As Elizabeth J. Church writes in *The Atomic Weight of Love* (2016), "it's difficult to resist the impulse to fill silence, to let the person you love off the hook, to let them be….a person struggling in life's paisley swirl of ugliness and blinding beauty."

Untangling the lives of my sister, mother, daughters, and myself is hard, but it's well past time. It is still hard for me not "to merge" intrusively, rather than to step back and take care of what's going on inside myself. Boundaries are important. My impulsiveness and selfishness still get me into trouble, but I do make an effort to moderate, if not make up for, my faults. Ben's lasting love has helped give me the confidence I need to accept myself as I am.

Ben proves to be stellar in filling in for our daughters when I can't. He can be there for them in ways that I haven't been. I know I "come first" for him in that he sees and appreciates and acknowledges who I am as no other ever has. He lets me relax in his love, something I wish for all my daughters, even though I acknowledge that the path to this place has not been easy, nor should it be. He comforts me at the same time that I know I need to rely on my own ability to comfort myself. At this time in my life I consider him a great luxury.

In the summer, I attended a workshop by Selena Fox on the mysteries of the oak tree. Taking a walk in Circle Sanctuary, I chose one oak upon which to meditate, noting that it had many dead branches on the way up. I likened these to what I'd sometimes thought were "dead ends" in my life: paths I'd thought I'd wanted but which didn't work out for me. If a tree does not grow alone, but in a copse or forest, it must grow within the confines and opportunities of its setting, and, as I had recently learned in a trip with Ben to California, the roots of redwoods are interwoven beneath the surface of the land, serving as supports for each other. Sometimes they withdraw into themselves, but at other times they communicate to help each other face threats or danger. Hopefully, it can be the same with families.

Back in Milwaukee, the recital went well and resulted in about $175 for the art venue. I made mistakes, but they didn't ruin the experience, which fulfilled my expectations, minimal as they had become. I was able to focus more on the music than on my fears. The forty people there seemed to appreciate my efforts. Listening to the CD later, I realized that I need to accept my current limits without letting them define me: to keep my identity loose, unfixed. Nevertheless, it is hard just to "be" when you know that something is coming to an end.

In a recent novel, the title of which unfortunately I can't remember, a Greek-American man who believes he will die in ten days tries to put his incredibly messy family life back together in that period of time. At some point he says something like, "I'm still alive so I must be allowed to make mistakes." Yes: mistakes are an allowance that is our wage for living. I like that. Mistakes propel us forward.

Slowly, with the help of my therapists, Ben, my teachers, my dreams, my daughters, my journal, and everyday life itself, I am learning to "tell the difference" between what I can and cannot control, what I should and should not do when it comes to "helping" others. It surprises me when I remember that Serenity Prayer on the wall of my mother's bedroom: "God grant me the serenity to accept the things I cannot change; the courage to change the things I can; and the wisdom to tell the difference."

My work at Marquette is over. Both the programs I've worked in for over thirty years, serving returning and/or under-represented students, have been shut down. The implications of this for our nation worry me, but, as I'm learning, I cannot control it.

For many years, perhaps because I've often felt like a "fish out of water," I've dreamed of trying to keep fish in a bowl of water when they seem intent on "escaping." I've always been afraid that they would die in the air, that I needed to "protect" them. Often, in my dreams, I have forgotten about them and neglected them. Recently, however, I dreamed of a "Gold" fish that was very content to be out of the water. Indeed, it was curious, companionable, and seemed well-suited to "breathe" in both air and water. Something in me has been transformed, perhaps alchemically.

The source of inequality between Ben and me—our unequal value as represented by our paychecks—has disappeared with our retirements. We celebrated his 70th birthday in a nearby resort town, and I wondered: when did things first change from my sensing our innate equality? when did I change from simply wanting to please him to fearing displeasing him? It still comes down, I believe, to who is seen as most important by society, what work, whose time, what achievements are seen as most important, as measured—mostly—by salary.

Feeling alone is not new to me. And yet I have resented people who have "left me": Marilyn, Jamie, Angela, and yes, Ben, during the times he worked in other states. As alone as I felt during all those years when he was working elsewhere, I knew that he was suffering too, in his own way. But now it is time to amend all resentments. Now we can linger over breakfast together, have time to deal with issues as they come up, laugh and relax. One day recently we were being playful in the kitchen while I was making dinner, and I told him to leave me alone. He turned me toward him, took me in his arms, and said: "I never want to leave you alone."

When he walked into his first radiation treatment that day, he said, "Well, this will be an adventure," and he was whistling Bruce Springsteen's song, "If I Should Fall Behind" (*Lucky Town*, 1992). The first verse goes like this:

> *We said we'd walk together baby come what may*
> *That come the twilight should we lose our way*
> *If as we're walking a hand should slip free*
> *I'll wait for you*
> *And should I fall behind*
> *Wait for me*

Epilogue

Yes: " A woman who lives long enough may finally be told she has done worthwhile work." But how much does age have to do with it? In 2019 I will have had 58 years longer than my sister, 22 years longer than Angela, and five years longer than my mother. It's true sometimes that age, especially after menopause, gives one the quiet time necessary to bring clarity to what one's life has meant. But not always for those of us who went straight from breast feeding to hot flashes. Nevertheless, the clarity of self-worth comes only in part from externals: how other people see you, whether your "work" is appreciated by others. Most of us need some acknowledgement. But if we live long enough, even that can fall away—the need for the praise and recognition of others, in whatever form. And if we are lucky—have our mind, most of our health, enough money not to have to worry about basic survival issues—we can ask *ourselves* what have we done with our "one wild and precious life," as Mary Oliver so famously put it. And, if we are another inch lucky, as we take stock, we are merciful: we will appreciate all we have been given and marvel at what we have made before we let it all go, along with "measuring sticks of all kinds/with their proud certainties" ("Baubo and Quantum Physics"). Like all creatures, we live and die. What remains is not our business.

As Bedatri D. Choudhury says in her essay, "Andy Goldsworthy's Ephemeral Art and Laborious Process, in a New Documentary,"

Goldsworthy incorporates death into the process of art making and celebrates the eternal kinetics of nature and seasons, so much so that he names such artworks Ephemeral Works. That is when he decides to photograph his artworks: to capture a moment, to freeze a memory in the forever-shifting dynamics of time and life. We see the yellowest of yellows and the greenest of greens frozen in photographs, as the camera hovers over the same trees, leaves, and grass as they quietly fade away. There is always a danger in seeing such transient artworks on screen, for the illusionary permanence that film offers. For viewers who haven't seen Goldsworthy's art change with time, the gaze of a [. . .] camera almost imparts a false stability to the works.

However, Goldsworthy's art is driven by an awareness of instability and mortality, which makes it a profound celebration of the present, of life. In one scene, he giddily lies down on the ground in the rain, leaving behind a dry outline of his body. He then walks away, knowing that the rain will fill his 'rain shadow,' yet doing it anyway, as if to prove that he was here — present yet at peace with the inescapability of erasure.

And yet…and yet…..I will close with Jane Hirshfield's necessary, opposing view (for what good is art without ambiguity and conflict?):

Only Tibetan monks and Native American elders create their art of happily scattered sand. For the rest, the sand is a sharp and alien intrusion that needs to be answered by layered, surrounding, lasting inpourings of pearl.
[. . .]To participate in the creative renewal of the world is as close as we may come to touching the cloth of

existence's original daybreak—in that moment, the artist is neither human nor god, neither perishable nor lasting, neither good nor bad. In that moment, when language has come awake, taken its seat in the full light of morning, and begun the tentative, much-crossed-out exploration or sure-tongued outpour, the artist is not even himself, herself. The artist and language and the page are given over to one thing alone—or rather, into no separable thing at all: they have surrendered the condition of noun to become fully verb. They are working. *And this working, the creative act of a whole and undivided being is the one true appetite of the writer's tongue and mind and heart, with us as long as the trout swims in the streambed while above it, slightly shadowing the surface, floats the faintest, curious glimmer of a watching human face.*

Theme and Variations for My Sister

theme:
Soon there will be no one
left
to remember you.

There will be no more
crones
to commune with your bones,

to stitch them together
again, yet
again, with silk thread.

So your bones will
dismember, and the embers
of your life (lived, unlived)

will wash downstream to
the mouth
of the ever-living earth.

No Isis will
gather
you in, no one will be

left to mourn except
the wind,
the wind.

var.1:
Soon
those who remember you
will also die.

No one
will eat and drink
in remembrance of you,

or wash
your body, or patch
a quilt with your dress.

The grace
of your crippled bones
—legs and hands—

will never
be recalled, nor
fantasies spun for the

long life
you might have lived.
I would gladly be your

Isis,
but am far
from immortal, leaving

the undying wind,
the south wind of Kansas
to chant, chant

enchant your tale.

var.2:
Soon Persephone will sink deep
into the dross of earth's
winter

and Demeter will fail to recall
even her grief in the
empty

fields of wheat. In Hades' realm
Persephone will reign,
still

queen of the dead with
no one to breathe her
story.

Splinters of youth, of
even the prospect
of blooms,

will scatter, the demented wind
unable to recount the spring
of its grief.

By the time May parts its buds,
I will be
gone.

var.3:
Feverish, so our mother's story goes,
your fingers drummed silent music

onto the pieced quilt.
Both pianist and drummer, you would seek

her estimation of a drum's tone:
was it not beautiful?

I went to the piano to transmute my grief
for a little while

when our father forbade me
to whisper your name.

Ever-loving sister, I have played
just one

secret song pieced together
from the scraps of your life.

Your fevered rhythm
is mine as well.
Is it not beautiful?

interlude:
We overwrite our stories with
the instruments given.

We complicate, riff, play with their fixed
strings, till our elaborate songs emerge,

in distorted cacophony.
Still, in the measured beat beneath
it all, flows the swift current of your name.

var. 4:
You were my teacher,
I your Magdalene, your
unsung disciple
who saw your body and said
you were not dead.

The tomb open, you
irreparably gone, my
bones ached. I was
and was not
you.

You ascended to Heaven.

I carefully gathered and stored
your relics.

You were gone in a flash.

I, cracked bell, have
told and told, had time to tell,
to tell,
re-tell.

var. 5:
I was the kid sister kicking your crippled leg,
wanting to make sure you were human.

Our mother asked, why couldn't I be more like you?
Revising is not easy: once again scanning the dark

dactyls of your name, rearranging, I wonder,
had you lived, would you have failed her too,

leaving her church and the life she picked out for you?
or would you have signed her contract?

Having a god for a sister is hard.
I am flawed, mortal, old.

This I have learned:
re-versing is not easy.

return to theme:
Soon there will be no one
left
to remember you,

      no apostle to stitch together the
      muddled remnants of your story.

My testament remains
your mummy, my only boon
against loss, its sarcophagus
sealed with my name.

Swiftly, the current will course
what's left of girl and crone
down to the mouth
of the ever-dying earth.

      Isis cannot gather us in.
      Nor can she mourn in her windless land.

In life, wind blows.
In life, we expire,
leaving our songs.

Is it not beautiful?

Chapter References

One:

Auden, W.H. *The Age of Anxiety* (Random House, 1947).

Chödrön, Pema. *Living Beautifully with Uncertainty and Change* (Shambhala, 2012).

Dale, Kathleen. "Family Snapshot." *The Beautiful Unnamed* (Zarigueya Press,2015).

Dooley, Thomas A. *The Edge of Tomorrow* (Farrar, Strauss, & Cudahy, 1958).

Eliot, T.S. *The Wasteland* (Liveright, 1922).

Friedan, Betty. *The Feminine Mystique* (W.W. Norton, 1963).

Palomar Observatory.

(https://en.wikipedia.org/wiki/Palomar_Observatory)

Smith, Betty. *A Tree Grows in Brooklyn* (Harper&Bros, 1943).

"The Most Dangerous Epidemics in US History."

(https://www.healthline.com/health/worst-disease-outbreaks-history)

Wilder, Thornton. *Our Town* (1939).

Two:

"Fraternity and Sorority History at OWU"
(https://www.owu.edu/alumni-and-friends/get-involved/fraternity-and-sorority-life-at-owu/fraternity-sorority-history-at-owu/

"Ohio Wesleyan University"
(https://en.wikipedia.org/wiki/Ohio_Wesleyan_University)

Steichen, Edward. *The Family of Man* (Museum of Modern Art/Macro Publishing, 1955).

Three:

Bonhoeffer, Dietrich. *Letters and Papers from Prison* (SCM Press, 1953).

Castaneda, Carlos. *The Teachings of Don Juan: A Yaqui Way of Knowledge* (U. of California Press, 1968).

O'Neill, George and Nena. *Open Marriage* (M. Evans & Co., 1972).

Our Bodies, Ourselves: A Book by and for Women . (Boston Women's Health Book Collective, 1970).

Roberts, Jane. *Seth Speaks: The Eternal Validity of the Soul* (Amber-Allen Pub. 1972).

Sainte-Marie, Buffy. "Until It's Time for You To Go" (Vanguard Records, 1967).

Seaman, Barbara. *The Doctors' Case against the Pill* (P.H. Wyden, 1969).

Simon, Carly. "Anticipation" (Universal Music Publishing Group, 1971).

UWM Libraries Archives (https://uwm.edu/libraries/archives/)

Four:

Aron, Elaine N. *The Highly Sensitive Person: How To Thrive when the World Overwhelms You* (Citadel Press, 1996).

Dale, Kathleen. "Adhesions." *Ties that Bind* (Finishing Line Press, 2006).

Gregoire, Carolyn and Scott Barry Kaufman. *Wired to Create: Unraveling the Mysteries of the Creative Mind* (Perigee, 2015).

Wilhelm, Richard and Cary Baynes (eds.). *I Ching: Or Book of Changes* (Bollinger Series xix, Princeton Univ. Press, 1950).

Five:

Bradshaw, John. *Homecoming: Reclaiming and Healing Your Inner Child* (Random House, 1992).

Hyde, Lewis. *The Gift: Creativity and the Artist in the Modern World* (Random House, 1983).

Lao Tsu. Gia-Fu Feng and Jane English, (trs.). *Tao Te Ching* (Vintage Books, 1972).

Ullmann, Liv. *Changing* (Knopf, 1977).

Six:

Dale, Kathleen. "Ghost." *Rescue Mission* (Antrim House Press, 2011).

Peckenpaugh, Angela J. *A Heathen Herbal* (Peaceable Press, 1986)

―――――――――――――――――-*Always Improving My Appetite* (Sackbut Press, 1994).

―――――――――――――――――― *Book of Charms* (Barnwood Press, 1983).

―――――――――――――――――-*Discovering the Mandala* (Lakes and Prairies Press, 1981)

―――――――――――――――――-*Letters from Lee's Army* (Morgan Press, 1979)

―――――――――――――――――-*Refreshing the Fey* (Sackbut Press, 1986)

―――――――――――――――――-*Remembering Rivers* (Sackbut Press, 1991)

―――――――――――――――――-*Singing a Circle of Seasons* (Sackbut Press, 1995)

―――――――――――――――――-*Who is the Jack?* (1973)

Seven:

Berends, Polly Berrien. *Whole Child/Whole Parent: A Spiritual and Practical Guide to the First Four Years of Parenthood* (Harpers' Magazine Press, 1975).

Dale, Kathleen. "Picking Peaches." *The Beautiful Unnamed* (Zarigueya Press, 2015).

Sexton, Anne. *Transformations* (Houghton & Mifflin, 1971).

Eight:

Adler, Margaret. *Drawing Down the Moon: Witches, Druids, Goddess-Worshippers, and Other Pagans in America Today* (Viking Press, 1979).

Dale, Kathleen. "Baubo Ponders Questions of Quantum Physics, part iii." *Avatars of Baubo* (Green Fuse Press, 2013).

Mariechild, Diane. *Mother Wit: A Feminist Guide to Psychic Development* (The Crossing Press, 1981).

Palmer, Parker J. *To Know as We Are Known: Education as a Spiritual Journey (*Harper Collins, 1983).

Spretnak, Charlene, ed. *The Politics of Women's Spirituality* (Anchor Press, 1982)

Starhawk. *The Spiral Dance: A Rebirth of the Ancient Religion of the Great Goddess* (Harper & Row, 1979).

Wheatley, Margaret J. *Leadership and the New Science: Discovering Order in a Chaotic World* (Berret Kohler Publishers, 1992).

Nine:

Dale, Kathleen. "Three Days at Lake Michigan: August, 1994." Previously unpublished.

Ten:

Briggs, John and F. David Peat. *Turbulent Mirror: An Illustrated Guide to Chaos Theory and the Science of Wholeness* (Harper & Row, 1989).

Castaneda, Carlos. *The Power of Silence: Further Teachings of Don Juan* (Washington Square Press, 1987).

Chopra, Deepak. *Path to Love: Spiritual Strategies for Healing* (Harmony Books, 1996).

Dale, Kathleen. "The Beautiful Unnamed." *The Beautiful Unnamed* (Zarigueya Press, 2015).

Eliot, T.S. *Four Quartets* (Harcourt, 1943).

Hawking, Stephen W. *A Brief History of Time: From the Big Bang to Black Holes* (Bantam Press, London. 1988).

Hillman, James. *The Soul's Code: In Search of Character and Calling* (Random House, 1996).

Hirshfield, Jane. *Ten Windows: How Great Poems Transform the World* (Alfred A Knopf, 2015).

Rilke, Rainer Marie. *Letters to a Young Poet* (Franz Xaver Kappus, 1929).

Sarton, May. *At Eighty-Two: A Journal* (W.W. Norton & Co. 1997).

Whitman, Walt. *Leaves of Grass* (Brooklyn, 1855).

Woodman, Marion. *Addiction to Perfection: The Still Unravished Bride, a Psychological Study* (Inner City Books, 1982).

Zwieg, Connie and Ben Wolf. *Romancing the Shadow: How to Access the Power Hidden in Our Dark Side* (Harper Collins, 1958).

Eleven:

Bolen, Jean Shinoda. *The Wise Woman Archetype: Menopause as Initiation* (Sounds True cassette, 2009).

Capra, Fritjhof. *The Web of Life: A Scientific Understanding of Living Systems* (Anchor Books, 1996).

Dale, Kathleen. "Baubo Wanders." *Avatars of Baubo* (Green Fuse Press, 2013).

Greene, Brian. *The Elegant Universe: Superstrings, Hidden Dimensions, and the Quest for the Ultimate Theory* (W.W.Norton, 1999).

Twelve:

Anthony, Carol K. *A Guide to the I Ching* (Anthony Publishing Co, 1980).

Dale, Kathleen. "directions for playing." *The Beautiful Unnamed* (Zarigueya Press, 2015).

Gallwey, W. Timothy. *The Inner Game of Tennis: The Classic Guide to the Mental Side of Peak Performance* (Random House, 1974).

Kingsolver, Barbara. *Pigs in Heaven* (Harper Collins, 1993).

Thirteen:

American Cancer Society. "The Limitations of Mammograms," 2017. (https://www.cancer.org/cancer/breast-cancer/screening-tests-and-early-detection/mammograms/limitations-of-mammograms.html)

McCall-Smith, Alexander. *Friends, Lovers, Chocolate* (Little, Brown; Pantheon, 2005).

Oliver, Mary. *What Do We Know: Poems and Prose Poems* (DeCapo, 2003).

Piercy, Marge. *To Be of Use* (Doubleday, 1973).

Roberts, Jane. *The God of Jane: A Psychic Manifesto* (Prentice-Hall, 1981).

Salinger, J.D. *Franny and Zooey* (Little and Brown, 1961).

Smith, Lee. *Oral History* (Ballantine, 1983).

Sondheim, Stephen. *Into the Woods* (first performed 1986, San Diego).

Wilbur, Richard. "For C." *Collected Poems 1943-2004* (Harcourt, 2004).

Wilhelm, Richard. "The Rainmaker." (https://psycheandnature.wordpress.com/tag/rainmaker/)

Williams, Terry Tempest. *When Women Were Birds: Fifty-Four Variations on Voice* (Macmillan, 2012).

Fourteen:

Dale, Kathleen. "Wild Rhubarb." *Malala: Poems for Malala Yousafzai,* ed. Hutchinson and Watson. (FutureCycle Press, 2013).

Gardner, Howard E. *Portraits Of Four Exceptional Individuals And An Examination Of Our Own Extraordinariness* (Perseus/Basic Books, 1997).

Goldsworthy, Andy. *Time* (Abrams, 2008).

Hyde, Lewis. *The Gift: Creativity and the Artist in the Modern World* (Penguin/Random House 1983).

Stevens, Wallace. *Letters of Wallace Stevens: Selected and Edited by Holly Stevens* (Knopf, 1972).

Fifteen:

Dale, Kathleen. "Palimpsest: Painting Her Again." (*Wisconsin People & Ideas Magazine*, Summer 2015.)

Finch, Annie (ed.) *A Formal Feeling Comes: Poems in Form by Contemporary Women* (Story Line Press, 1994).

Hirsch, Edward. *Gabriel: A Poem* (Knopf, 2014).

Pym, Barbara. *Jane and Prudence* (Pan Books, 1953).

Sixteen:

Dale, Kathleen. "Survivor: Banking on It" *Rescue Mission* (Antrim House Press, 2011).

——————————"Depth Perception." *Rescue Mission* (Antrim House Press, 2011).

——————————"when you leave me." *Rescue Mission* (Antrim House Press, 2011).

French, Marilyn. *In the Name of Friendship* (The Feminist Press at CUNY, 2008).

Glück, Louise. *The Wild Iris* (Harper Collins Ecco,1992).

Graham, Jorie. *Overlord* (Harper Collins, 2005).

——————————. *The Dream of the Unified Field: Selected Poems 1974-1994* (Harper Collins Ecco (2002).

Shulman, Alix Kates. *Drinking the Rain: A Memoir* (North Point Press, 2004).

Williams, C.K. *The Singing* (Farrar, Straus and Giroux, 2003).

Seventeen:

Dale, Kathleen. "Patchwork". *The Beautiful Unnamed* (Zarigueya Press, 2015).

Walker, Alice. "Everyday Use." *In Love and Trouble* (Rutgers University Press, 1973).

Eighteen:

Dale, Kathleen. "The Craft." *The Beautiful Unnamed* (Zarigueya Press, 2015).

Haupt, Lyanda. *Crow Planet: Essential Wisdom from the Urban Wilderness* (Little, Brown, and Company, 2009).

L'Engle, Madeleine. *A Wrinkle in Time* (Ariel Books, 1962).

Levin, Rami. "Passages." *Moods: Piano Music by American Women Composers.*
Max Lifschitz, piano (www.northsouthmusic.org 2008).

Mosley, Walter. *The Thrill Is Gone* (Orion Publishing Group, 2011).

Shenk, David. *The Genius in All of Us: Why Everything You've Been Told about Genetics, Talent, and IQ is Wrong* (Penguin/Random House, 2010).

Viola, Frank. *From Eternity to Here: The Quest for the Ultimate Theory of Time* (Dutton, 2009).

Nineteen:

Dale, Kathleen. "Sit. Stay." *Rescue Mission* (Antrim House Press, 2011).

Twenty:

Dale, Kathleen. "At Seventy." *The Beautiful Unnamed* (Zarigueya Press, 2015).

———————————illus.by Lily Duermeier. *Deconstruction Zone* (http://www.lulu.com/shop/kathleen-dale/deconstruction-zone/paperback/product-18861003.html).

Endicott, Marina. *Good to a Fault* (Harper Collins, 2008).

Greene, Brian. *The Hidden Reality: Parallel Universes and the Deep Laws of the Cosmos* (Macmillan, 2011).

Hadley, Tessa. *The London Train* (Harper Perennial, 2011).

Harrison, Jim. *The River Swimmer* (Grove Press, 2014).

Herbert, George. "The Flower." *The Temple* (1633).

Hirshfield, Jane. *Ten Windows: How Great Poems Transform the World* (Alfred A Knopf, 2015).

Klein, Daniel Martin and Thomas Cathcart. *Heidegger and a Hippo Walk through the Pearly Gates* (Viking Adult, 2009).

Olds, Sharon. *Stag Leap* (Knopf, 2012).

Penny, Louisa. *Bury Your Dead* (Macmillan, 2010).

Tierny, John. "Do You Have Free Will? Yes, It's the Only Choice" *The New York Times* (https://www.nytimes.com/2011/03/22/science/22tier.html)

Twenty-one:

Arsenault, Emily. *Miss Me When I'm Gone* (William Morrow, 2012).

Church, Elizabeth J. *The Atomic Weight of Love* (Algonquin, 2016).

Jahren, Hope. *Lab Girl: A Memoir* (Knopf, 2017).

Smith, Lee. *Dimestore: A Writer's Life* (Algonquin, 2017).

Springsteen, Bruce. "If I Should Fall Behind" (Alfred Publishing Co., 1992).

Tartt, Donna. *The Goldfinch* (Little Brown &Co. 2015).

Epilogue:

Choudhury, Bedatri D. "Andy Goldsworthy's Ephemeral Art and Laborious Process in a New Documentary." 2016. (https://hyperallergic.com/431625/andy-goldsworthy-documentary-leaning-into-the-wind/)

Dale, Kathleen. "Theme and Variations." Previously Unpublished.

Hirshfield, Jane. *Ten Windows: How Great Poems Transform the World* (Alfred A Knopf, 2015).

Oliver, Mary. "The Summer Day." *House of Light* (Beacon Press, 1990).

About the Author

A Pushcart nominee for her award-winning poetry, Kathleen A. Dale is the author of four books of poetry. She was nominated for inclusion in Best American Poetry 2014, and has been featured poet in many journals. She is a serious amateur pianist and sees an intimate connection between music and poetry.

Born in Kansas, she has lived on the shore of Lake Michigan for many years with her husband. They have three grown daughters.

Dale holds a Doctorate in Modern American Poetry and for many years taught writing courses for non-traditional and returning adult college students. Today she mentors private poetry clients and is a free-lance editor. See her website at **kathleenanndale.com**.

Made in the USA
Columbia, SC
16 March 2019